One couldn't ask for a better guide through the competing loyalties of faith, family, and work at the highest levels of a major corporation. Diane Paddison has remarkable narrative skills. It is easy to see why she is a corporate superstar. This is the vulnerable inside story of corporate life competing with faith and family. I highly recommend this book.

Bob Buford
former Chairman, Buford Television, Inc.
author, *Halftime* and *Finishing Well*
Founder and Chairman, Leadership Network

Diane Paddison's book provides rare firsthand insight into the joys and tensions of balancing family, faith, and career with transparency and deep reflection. In this book, leaders of companies, churches, and other organizations will find new insights on how to make their community more conducive to professional women.

Kevin J. Jenkins
President and CEO, World Vision

Professional Christian woman, how long will you juggle your faith, household, husband, kids, and career without a road map? Diane Paddison's beautiful, entertaining, and fascinating book offers everything you need to find balance, fulfillment, and yes, peace.

Miles McPherson
Senior Pastor, The Rock Church, San Diego

I fervently wish *Work, Love, Pray* had been available when I was twenty-eight and struggling between the worlds of corporate, church, sports, and relationships. *Work, Love, Pray* can help every young professional woman come to know these truths decades earlier than I did—that God wires us to be who we are and puts us right where we are supposed to be in order to develop, contribute, and grow closer to him.

Linda Lindquist Bishop
President, Courageous Thinking Inc.

Work, Love, Pray is a new and deeply significant guide for Christian women on their journey to leadership. "Faith, family, and career" are wonderfully balanced in this remarkable resource.

Frances Hesselbein
President and CEO, Leader to Leader Institute

This book captures the secret of the fundamental strength that all women, consciously or unconsciously, are seeking. It appears to me that the successful, enterprising women, depicted here, realized early on that they needed help and the presence of the Lord at all times. *Work, Love, Pray* is a gem of practical advice.

Norma A. Coldwell
former Dean of Women Students, SMU
former Head of Risk, 65 Latin American countries, Riggs Bank

In Diane Paddison's *Work, Love, Pray*, she lays out great advice on how young women can find balance in their lives and manage the many conflicts that face us all as we consider our priorities and how to keep them in check. I have seen up close how Diane has managed her faith, her family, and her career — all with tremendous passion and energy. Her insights are practical and on target — and this book is a road map to an abundant, productive, and meaningful life.

Mike Lafitte
President, Americas, CB Richard Ellis

Diane Paddison provides great insight and advice on how to reach for success without sacrificing what's most important to you. In *Work, Love, Pray*, Paddison does a remarkable job of articulating the challenges that young, aspiring women face as they navigate the waters of balancing a family and a career while staying true to their moral compass.

Charlotte Anderson
Chair of the National Advisory Board, Salvation Army
Executive Vice President, Brand Management/
President of Charities, Dallas Cowboys Club

PRACTICAL WISDOM FOR YOUNG
PROFESSIONAL CHRISTIAN WOMEN

work
love
pray

diane paddison

ZONDERVAN.com/
AUTHORTRACKER
follow your favorite authors

ZONDERVAN

Work, Love, Pray
Copyright © 2011 by Diane Detering-Paddison

This title is also available as a Zondervan ebook. Visit www.zondervan.com/ebooks.

This title is also available in a Zondervan audio edition. Visit www.zondervan.fm.

Requests for information should be addressed to:

Zondervan, *Grand Rapids, Michigan 49530*

Library of Congress Cataloging-in-Publication Data

Paddison, Diane, 1959-
    Work, love, pray : practical wisdom for young professional Christian women / Diane
Paddison.
       p. cm.
    Includes bibliographical references.
    ISBN 978-0-310-33137-7 (softcover)
    1. Businesswomen—Religious life. 2. Women employees—Religious life. 3.
Work—Religious aspects—Christianity. 4. Businesswomen—Conduct of life. 5.
Christian women—Religious life. I. Title.
  BV4596.B8P33 2011
  248.8'43—dc22   2011012872

Cover design: Faceout Studio
Cover photography: Faceout Studio | Paul Nielson
Interior design: Matthew Van Zomeren

Printed in the United States of America

11 12 13 14 15 16 17 18 /DCI/ 22 21 20 19 18 17 ·16 15 14 13 12 11 10 9 8 7 6 5 4 3 2 1

To my husband, Chris;
my children, Opie and Annie;
my stepchildren, Rose and Gus;
my parents, Roger and Sharon Detering.
Without God, none of this would have been possible.

contents

foreword

WHEN DIANE PADDISON ASKED ME to write the foreword for her book, *Work, Love, Pray*, I was delighted and honored. Recently a good friend introduced us, and within the first few minutes of our meeting, Diane and I quickly realized that we share similar avocations. We have achieved successful careers, are involved in women's issues, have a desire to make an impact in people's lives, and most importantly, we both have a strong faith in God. So, when Diane described the premise of *Work, Love, Pray*, I was eager to read it and wholeheartedly acknowledged the need for a book that reminds women that God has strategically placed us in the workforce. He wants us to utilize the gifts and abilities He has granted us to accomplish His purpose in our lives.

Diane and I talked about the way God has worked in our lives. He assuredly has equipped us with unique talents and perseverance to achieve success. But it is also strikingly apparent that God has opened doors of opportunity for us. Though in different businesses — Diane as a chief operating officer of multiple Fortune 500 real estate companies, and me serving at The White House for both President and Mrs. Bush, then as the deputy chief of protocol of the United States, and now in Dallas at The Bush Institute — the Lord clearly has a purpose for our lives ... and He has a purpose for yours as well.

The following two verses are great reminders that God has a plan for each of us: Proverbs 16:9 says, "We can make our plans, but the Lord determines our steps," and Jeremiah 29:11 says, "For I know the plans I have for you, declares the Lord, plans to prosper you and not to harm you, plans to give you a hope and a future." God has a specific plan for your life and mine. When we trust in Him and walk closely with Him, He will open doors of opportunity for us that we could never open ourselves. He gives us favor. When thinking about my own life, I am overwhelmed by God's goodness, faithfulness, and favor. In 2000, I started working as a volunteer for then-Governor Bush's campaign for president in my home state of California. I did not have any connections to the Bushes, the Republican Party, nor anyone who worked for them. But I worked diligently and did any task needed, from taking the garbage out to driving President Bush's nephew to events. I quickly was given more important responsibilities because of my strong work ethic and availability to work long days. But looking back, it is evident that the Lord lifted me up and gave me favor. One day, Governor Bush was coming to Los Angeles for events. The volunteer who was supposed to help with the event got the stomach flu, so I was asked to help the advance team coordinate the governor's visit. One of the advance representatives needed help assembling press packets and photocopying press kits. In order to complete the task, it meant that I had to miss Governor Bush's speech, which was disappointing, but the job had to get done. As we ran the press kits out to the press bus, I actually got to meet Governor Bush (a little blessing from God). And because of my dedication, I was asked to help with the following day's events. Soon after, Governor Bush won the primary in California and I flew to Austin in hopes of landing a job on the campaign. When I went to the campaign office, I saw the woman I had helped in California a few months earlier. She was in Austin for only one day—and it happened to be the day I was visiting. She gave my resume to the director of advance that day, and a few days later, I received a call to join the campaign full-time as an advance representative. Looking back, I am still amazed at how the Lord opened doors I could not have opened for myself. In those early years, I never imagined the Bushes would even know my name. But today, I have traveled to over sixty countries with them, regularly have dinner in their home, and work closely with them at the Bush Institute. I tell this story to illustrate one of the principles that Diane lays out in the book—that when our faith is the center of our lives, the Lord will open doors to us, give us supernatural favor, and use us to influence others.

As Diane points out in the book, women have more opportunities than ever before—more women are graduating from college than men, a record number of women are in the workforce, and women are getting married and having children later than ever before in history. While women have an abundance of opportunities, we are also faced with the challenge of balancing our lives—work, family, personal lives, health, faith ... and the list goes on. God uniquely made women to multitask, but many of us feel incredible pressure. Expectations for women at this time in history can cause confusion about our role and anxiety about how to balance it all.

Work, Love, Pray is a fantastic book for women who desire to thrive in EVERY area of their lives. Diane provides practical tools for women, especially those in the workforce, who want to learn how best to balance faith, work, and family. She includes personal stories from her own life that provide insights from which the reader can glean important principles for their lives.

I am confident you will find *Work, Love, Pray* inspiring and encouraging. Use the stories and tools provided in the book to help you on your journey. Most importantly, remember God has a plan and purpose for you. When you reflect back, I believe you will see God's hand in your life every step of the way. When we stay close to God, we never know the exciting places He will take us. This book will prepare you to go.

Blessings,
Charity N. Wallace
Director, Women's Initiative at the George W. Bush
Institute, and senior advisor to Mrs. Laura Bush

introduction

WHEN I GRADUATED FROM COLLEGE, I did what every college graduate does: I looked for a job. I mean a real job. I'd done all sorts of jobs on the family fruit farm near Harrisburg, Oregon, from managing the peach-picking crews to picking up rotten fruit in the orchard to operating the cash register at our roadside fruit stand. Now I was ready to go to work in a business suit and carry a briefcase. I can't say I really thought in terms of "career." That seemed like something older people did. I just wanted a job that would give me a salary and a chance to use what I had learned in college.

Fortunately, I found just such a job. Although I grew up in a relatively conservative home, I was given tremendous encouragement to hop out of the comfortable nest my parents had built for me and fly off into the world of opportunity that stretched ahead of me. Unlike previous generations of Christian women who went to college to get their Mrs. degree, it was just assumed in our household that I would go to college, get a degree, and find a good job. And that's exactly what I did.

What I *wasn't* prepared for, however, was how to manage my job with two other things that were very important to me: my faith in God and, eventually, a husband and children. During the first couple years out of college, it was just my job, my little apartment, and me. If I had to work late, I didn't have to call anyone and let them know where I was. Those

13

were great years where I learned so much about the corporate world and my own strengths and abilities. But it wasn't long before my job became a career. If it hasn't happened to you yet, it will. You start out taking whatever job comes along that's even loosely related to your college major. Because you are a reasonably intelligent person with a strong work ethic, you find your stride quickly and earn that first promotion. You get a bit of that adrenaline rush that comes from doing a job well and being recognized by your peers and supervisor, which motivates you to stretch a little further, and before you know it, you've been given greater responsibilities. What started out as a cool way to pay off your college loans or save for graduate school is now a full-fledged career. You enjoy what you do, you're pretty good at it, and life seems pretty nice.

That's exactly how I felt when I found myself partway up the ladder at Trammell Crow, one of the world's largest real-estate companies. I'd been out of college for nine years, including two years of graduate school. By this time I had met my husband, and conventional wisdom in some circles would suggest I no longer needed to work. Now I need to be very clear about something. I think it's wonderful that many women are able to enjoy fulfilling lives as stay-at-home moms and homemakers. I know and admire a number of women who are well educated and capable of making their marks in the workplace but have chosen to stay home for a variety of good reasons. At the same time, I realize that not every woman has that choice. For many families today, two incomes are necessary to afford a reasonable standard of living and still be able to set aside some money for future college expenses. But in cases like my own, some women are the primary breadwinners. I felt that God had prepared me to enter the business world, where I could honor him as a professional Christian woman.

So for more than twenty years, I've been doing my best to grow in my career, keep the fire burning in my marriage, help my kids with their homework and attend their school and sporting events, and remain close to the God I love. I'd like to say that I've managed to balance all of that gracefully all of the time, but I haven't. There have been times when I felt that balancing the Big Three—family, faith, and career—was impossible. Things would be going great at work, but my home life was falling apart. And when it came to faith, I soon learned that most churches don't quite know what to do with a woman who couldn't attend the 10:00 a.m. women's Bible study because she was giving a presentation in a conference room two thousand miles away. I don't consider myself a feminist, but I'll have to admit it bugged me when I was asked to bring a dish to a church function while the men were asked to serve on the finance committee. I can whip up a casserole as well as anyone, but I've also negotiated a few multi-million-dollar deals and managed a $600 million business, so why stick me with the tuna and noodles? I'm almost ashamed to admit that there were times when I didn't feel as if I was part of a church because the disconnect was so great, and it was experiences like that which led me to write this book.

For my generation of Christian women (I like to consider myself in the *very* early years of midlife), I was somewhat of a pioneer. Many women worked until they started a family and then took the next twenty years off to stay home as professional moms. But for you and other young Christian women, that may not be a popular option, largely because of the financial realities of most families, greater access to reliable childcare, and increasing opportunities for women in the workplace.

If you're single, you've probably already discovered that your church's and your family's primary mission is to help you find a spouse. There's certainly nothing wrong with finding the right man if you desire to get married, but the young, single Christian women I talk to want church to be more. They want to grow in their faith and reap the benefits of worshipping God with other believers, but too often they just quit being part of a church family because they feel so out of place there.

If you're married, you may have already begun to rub up against some of the tensions that come with two incomes, two careers. Who handles the family finances? What do you do if your job requires a fair amount of travel and your husband is uncomfortable with it? What happens if one of you enjoys success and promotions while the other one struggles?

introduction

Enter children, and things can get complicated real fast. Which of you adjusts your schedule to make it to Rose's recital? Which one of you negotiates a flex-time agreement with your employer to allow for a later starting time or an earlier departure time at the office? And after both of you rush around to your kids' school events and then go back to the office to finish a project, when do you find time just for each other? How do you have a quiet time of personal devotions and prayer when every waking minute of your day is spoken for? And even though I've always gone to church on Sundays, many young women have begun to wonder why they should spoil the one day of the week when they can sleep in.

I don't have all the answers to these and other questions you're bound to face as a young professional Christian woman, but I've walked in your shoes and know what it's like to try to have a career without sacrificing your family or your faith. I've learned some things the hard way and might be able to help you avoid some of the pitfalls that are ahead of you. But more than anything, I want to be a voice of encouragement whispering in your ear, "You can do it!"

I believe in what you're doing. I know the impact you can have on the world as you live out your faith and values alongside your colleagues. Whether you're a doctor or a school teacher, a lawyer or a business leader, I believe God put you where you are for a purpose. He gave you skills, talent, and knowledge that enable you to contribute to society through a career that he also provided for you. I know you want to honor him in all you do at work, in your home, and in your community, and I realize that sometimes it all seems so daunting. I know because even as I sat at my desk as the chief operating officer of two global corporations, I would wonder if this was where God wanted me to be. If it was just too much to try to be a good mom and wife *and* have a career. As always, his answer was clear: this is exactly where I want you to be.

So pour yourself a cup of coffee and settle into a nice big comfortable chair while I start our journey together with a story.

dream job

THE CALL CAME OUT OF THE BLUE.

"Diane, would you like to come work for us?"

It was a guy I knew from my time at Harvard Business School, and though we weren't real close, we had stayed in touch over the years because we were in the same industry. Three years earlier, he had been named the CEO of a major real-estate company with a global presence. He was calling because he needed to replace a key member of his leadership team.

"Why, John, that's awfully nice of you to think of me, but I'm very happy where I am right now," I replied.

I wasn't being coy or trying to play hard to get. It was true. I had just completed a twenty-two-year run with one of the nation's biggest commercial real-estate companies and really had no reason to leave. I had started out as a broker and eventually found myself as the chief operating officer and president of global services for my company.

I can't say that I set out to climb so high, but then again I was always the kid in school who tried to be the best at everything, so I guess you could say I just carried that competitive spirit with me when I started working. But I also had the good fortune of working for a company that embraced diversity and gave women the same opportunity to succeed that they gave men. At the time of John's call, I presided over a $600 million division of the company, with 4,500 employees who provided real-estate outsourcing services to eighty-five of the Fortune 100 companies. I had been a part of the ten-member executive team that sold our company to another company, quadrupling our size and providing even greater opportunities for me to grow. I absolutely loved what I was doing at the time.

Other Considerations

But there was another reason I really wasn't looking to leave my company. Throughout my tenure I was always given the flexibility to grow as an employee without sacrificing my family or my faith. From the very beginning I knew the risks of going to work as a professional. Whether it's the world of business, law, education, medicine — it doesn't matter. The work world has a way of demanding so much of you that there's little left over for other things that may be important to you. I had seen how long hours and too much travel, combined with the stress of trying to succeed, kept many men from their families, and I didn't want that to happen to me. So when I went to work for this company, I shared openly with them my commitment to my family and my faith and was thrilled to learn that from the CEO on down, these values were shared. If I had a major presentation to make and I got a call from school telling me that one of my kids was sick, it was never an issue: "Go take care of your family, Diane. I'll fill in for you, or we can reschedule the meeting."

Why would I want to leave a great job like that?

John must have known something of my competitive nature, because he began pushing all the right buttons.

"Well, Diane, currently you're the president of the global-services business of a $4 billion market cap company. How would you like to be the chief operating officer of a $16 billion market cap company?"

Hmmm. That got my attention.

"Not only that, but we have operations in twelve countries, with plans to expand into others. We're growing like crazy, and you'd have an integral role in our future growth."

I was beginning to imagine myself in that new role, envisioning what I could do with their resources, and some of the things I would do to improve their efficiency. Plus, I have to admit, as much as I liked my current job, there's something exciting about new challenges. I had just finished a major project related to the merger of our company, and I had my successor ready, so if there was a good time for a transition, this was it. Still, I wasn't quite sure this was the right thing for me at the time, but as we talked on the phone, I agreed to meet with John to discuss it further. So a few days later, he flew to Dallas and we had dinner. At one point he pulled out a manila folder from his briefcase, opened it, set it down beside me, and asked, "Would this entice you to come work for us?"

I tried not to look surprised, but I'm sure my jaw dropped. It was the compensation package he was offering me, and let's just say it was a lot more money than I was currently making, with a stock option package that made it even more attractive. When all was said and done, it was almost triple what I was currently making. I have never made money the sole factor in deciding whom to work for, but this was awfully tempting.

I began thinking about how I could do a better job of providing for my family, when it suddenly hit me. As much as my family would benefit from the bigger salary, what they've always really needed—and what I've always wanted to be able to give them—was me! I had been so fortunate in my current company to be able to grow and succeed while still being able to attend their school events and be home by 6:00 p.m. If I couldn't be assured of the same type of flexible work arrangement, no amount of money could lure me away. So I took a big gulp and spoke up—not for more money or a bigger bonus, but for my family.

"John, I need to be up front with you. There are some things that are more important to me than anything—even more important to me than the company I work for or the money I make."

I then shared with him my commitment to my family, to my marriage, and to my faith. I told him that since my children were well established with friends and good schools in Dallas, I couldn't move to the company's headquarters in Denver. I explained to him how important it was for me to be a part of a church family. I shared with him how I would never let the responsibilities of a job interfere with my marriage. Much to my surprise, he didn't back away from his initial offer and in fact affirmed these personal commitments. I knew John to be a man of his word, but I insisted that my contract include specific assurances that I could arrange my work schedule around my family's schedules, that overnight travel would be limited to one night a week on average, and that my international travel would be limited to five weeklong trips per year. In addition, I could continue to live in Dallas until my daughter graduated from high school.

When John agreed that all of my requests would be included in my contract, I really couldn't find any reason not to accept his offer. It wasn't a dream job for me, but it was close. In our discussions about my role, it became clear that they needed the skill set that I would bring to the job, and there's nothing quite as energizing as knowing that what you are doing is helping your company grow. Furthermore, this was a company with whom my current company had done business, so I already knew several people on the leadership team. In fact, the chief financial officer used to report quarterly to me as the president of a company that was a major provider to Trammell Crow Company/CB Richard Ellis. I thought he was a fine man with whom I had talked about our families, and I knew about his faith. It would be great to work alongside him again, knowing there was at least one other person on the leadership team who shared my priorities. The company was entering a period of rapid growth, expanding into new countries, and I thrived on the organizational and structural challenges that this would present. Plus, I wouldn't have to relocate, I would be home for dinner at night, and as an added bonus, I would be able to visit my oldest son, who attended college in Boulder, when I had to be at the company's headquarters in Denver.

As I said, not my dream job, but close. Close enough that I accepted John's offer. I'll never forget my first flight to Denver to meet my team. As the plane lifted off the runway and I watched the Dallas skyline disappear in the distance, it was so comforting to know I would be home the next day and that I had found another company that supported my values of faith and family. My former company had been great about my decision to leave, even going the extra mile in allowing me to work for another real-estate company despite a noncompete clause in my contract. As I reached into my briefcase for some papers to go over, I said a little prayer of thanks for the way God's hand was present in every detail of this transition, and about an hour later, I walked into the headquarters of my new company. I spent the next two months commuting to Denver from Dallas and making the occasional trip to one of our other offices around the globe. My new colleagues were great to work with, and not once did John pressure me to break any of the "family clauses" of my contract.

Falling Fast

That was in June 2008. By about September of that same year, the economic downturn at home and abroad started to make its presence known in my new company. Having slogged through the recession of 2001, I wasn't particularly alarmed. I figured we would take our hits on the bottom line just like everyone else, but that eventually we would pull out of it and be an even stronger company. I began making the necessary adjustments in my area and prepared for the general belt-tightening that comes with a sluggish economy. Unfortunately, things got worse. You've heard the expression "The bigger they are, the harder they fall." We were a pretty big company, and we were falling fast. When I reported for duty in June, our stock price was around sixty dollars per share. As we approached our November board-of-directors meeting that same year, the stock price had fallen to under twenty dollars. As a member of the leadership team, I felt that we had prepared an excellent plan to present to the board of directors that mapped out our strategy for recovery, but

I'd been in the business world long enough to know what was about to happen. Sure enough, after our presentation to the board, my good friend John who had hired me—the CEO of our company—left. That's just the way it happens in business.

In one of life's little ironies, the new CEO used to be the COO, whom I replaced! You might think that would have put my job at risk—or at least create some awkwardness between us—but he was a wonderful Christian gentleman, and we got off to a great start. At the same time, he had a huge job ahead of him and not much time to do it. He knew that if he didn't turn things around quickly, we might not last. As a measure of his character, guess who he worked with to handle an extremely critical sale of one of our overseas operations: John, the former CEO. And the resulting deal poured a lot of cash back into our company.

But of course we needed a lot more cash to right the ship. By that time, a team under my leadership identified $.37 per share in cost cutting. I've never been one to shy away from a challenge, but increasingly the stress of trying to meet the demands of my job began to bleed over into my family life, something I had worked all my life to avoid. There were many times when I knew I could get a lot more done and be a "real member" of the executive team if I stayed longer at my office in Denver, but I wasn't ready to pay that price. I can't tell you how many times I was on the phone in my kitchen trying to solve problems with my staff as I shoved dinner in the oven or used that unique "mom's sign language" to let one of my kids know I'd be off the phone in ten minutes.

In spite of the almost frantic pace of work, I managed to keep things balanced pretty well, and when I had to stay in Denver longer than I liked, my husband, Chris, was able to adjust his own work schedule to stay home with the kids. We've always taken that approach whenever one of us is going through a stressful season at work, and I knew it would be just a matter of time before things got back to normal. We supported each other in many different hardships, and Chris always pulled through when I couldn't. I'm not saying it was easy, but this is part of the trade-off if you're a professional. I was just hoping that normal would return soon, but until it did, I would put up with the craziness.

"We Need to Talk"

As I said, my new boss, the CEO, was a great guy who shared my faith and understood my commitment to my family. I was confident he would have us back on top of our game soon, which encouraged me to continue finding ways to reduce expenses and further develop our global focus on the operations side of our business. In other words, I could see the light at the end of the tunnel and anticipated the better days I knew were ahead. From earlier experiences, I knew how rewarding it was to go through a difficult period and come out on the other side in a stronger position. What I didn't know at the time, however, was how much it would cost me personally.

I had sent the new CEO my plan for 2009 and wanted to get his agreement on my goals and priorities. That prompted a response: "Diane, we need to talk."

I pretty much knew what was coming. I was the COO of the company. I lived in Dallas, while the rest of my team worked out of our Denver office and in a culture that wasn't virtual. While the rest of the leadership team was being dispatched all over the globe to put out fires and manage our recovery plan, I managed to be home for dinner and be with my church family on the weekends. I didn't really feel guilty about being able to work the way I was, because it was part of my contract with the company. I never would have gone to work for them if they hadn't allowed me the flexibility to have a fairly normal family life. And even though I wasn't traveling as much as my colleagues, I was doing a good job and adding value to the company.

However, when I signed that contract, the company was in great shape. Now it was in trouble. The person with whom I had negotiated that contract no longer ran the company. My boss wasted little time.

"Diane, I know we have a contract, but I need more of you. It's not that you're not doing your job, but I need you here in Denver. It's just not working with you being in Dallas."

For twenty-three years I'd been able to manage my family, my faith, and my career. And now for the first time I was being asked to put my career ahead of everything else. It's one thing to *say* that your family and your faith are more important to you than your career. Values are easy to hold when they're never challenged. But when push comes to shove, you learn whether they really *are* the guiding priorities of your life. I loved the work I was doing for this company, having taken the position of global chief operating officer. They rewarded me well for my work, with a more than adequate salary and good annual bonuses, plus nice stock options.

But they weren't family. They weren't a teenage daughter who still needed a mom around at night. They weren't a teenage son struggling to make good choices in his life. As much as I could rationalize accepting my boss's decision and moving to Denver, I ultimately turned to him and agreed that it was best for me to leave the company. And I haven't once regretted being true to my personal convictions, even though it meant losing a job I enjoyed.

I chose to open the book with this story because it shows quite dramatically everything that's going to come at you at one time or another in your professional career: opportunity, tragedy, conflicting values. As a young professional woman, you may have already encountered some mind-bending challenges at home or at work that make you question your ability, your sanity, or both! In the rest of the book, we'll look at where we've come from, where we're headed, and how to keep our lives—professional, personal, and spiritual—on track.

For Reflection or Discussion

1. Describe your dream job—either one that you already have or one that you wish you could have.
2. What would you be willing to give up in order to have your dream job? Would you be willing to relocate? Would you take a cut in pay?

3. Many men in their forties and fifties have high-paying jobs that they hate, but they stay because of the money and security. It's called "golden handcuffs." Could you ever see this happening to you? Why or why not?

4. What are your deal breakers—those things that would keep you from taking a job or that would cause you to quit a job?

5. When you have a major decision to make, how do you go about making it?

Why People Quit Their Jobs

Even during an economic recession, people leave their jobs voluntarily. According to the U.S. Bureau of Labor Statistics, more people quit their jobs in March 2010 than were laid off. Barbara Safani, executive coach and owner of Career Solvers (www.careersolvers.com), lists the top ten reasons people quit their jobs.

1. They were underemployed.
2. They were stretched to their limit.
3. They were recruited with a better opportunity.
4. They couldn't stand their boss.
5. The job stress was killing them.
6. They were bored to tears.
7. The company was struggling.
8. They were offered a voluntary package.
9. Their life changed.
10. They started their own business.

farm girl

I WAS FIVE YEARS OLD WHEN I GOT MY FIRST JOB.

I'm not kidding.

My grandfather's farm stretched over four hundred acres of fertile Oregon countryside that grew the sweetest, juiciest fruit on the planet. Rhubarb. Cherries. Peaches. Pears. Apples. And the vegetables. Row upon row of bright red tomatoes, summer squash, green peppers, cucumbers, and more. My grandfather and father pretty much ran the farm together, and when I turned five, they must have thought it was time I joined the other hired hands. They started me out at the fruit stand down by the road where we sold our produce.

I'll never forget getting up early in the morning my first day on the job and walking with my father to my grandfather's shed, which was sort of the headquarters for the whole operation. There everyone got their assignments and then headed off into the fields or, in my case, to the fruit stand. And even though I was just a kid, this wasn't merely a cute little diversion to keep me entertained for the summer. My dad and grandfather weren't into cute.

One of my jobs at the fruit stand was to make boxes. In the back of the stand we had these big stacks of flattened cardboard boxes that had to be opened and folded and then stapled to turn them into boxes for the various fruits and vegetables. Not so easy for a five-year-old, but I kept at it until I got pretty good. Of course, the pay made it all worthwhile: my grandfather gave me a nickel for each box I made.

Sadly, my grandfather passed away during my second summer of working for him. We were all right there when it happened. He was carrying a box of fruit, then set it down and had a heart attack. He never recovered. Of course we were all sad, but all of my aunts, uncles, and cousins in the area immediately came over and worked the fruit stand so my grandma and dad could take care of the funeral arrangements. Even though they had never worked at the stand before, they just took over and learned on the job so that the rest of us wouldn't have to work.

Being so young, I got a bit of a break and only worked about four to five hours a day. But around the time I turned eight, I must have qualified as a grown-up because I not only put in a good eight to nine hours a day; I graduated to the fields where, depending on the time of the year, I thinned the fruit off the trees, weeded the row crops, or helped with the harvest. We would start around seven in the morning and usually worked until five in the evening. Once the fruit stand opened, I sometimes worked there until seven at night. Child labor at its best, but it taught me so much.

Farm-Fresh Management Training

To this day, I'm pretty good at math, thanks to having to use it so much on the farm. When I graduated to the fields, one of my first jobs was to assist with the rhubarb harvest. Workers would pull the rhubarb stalks out of the ground, cut the leaves off the top with a sharp knife and trim the other end, and then throw the bright red fruit into a big wooden crate. Then one of the men would put the crate onto the scales and call out the weight. My job was to record the weight on a produce ticket, but first I had to mentally subtract 18 pounds, which was what the box itself weighed. And I had to do it fast. So someone would call out "103 pounds!" and I had to quickly write down 85. Talk about pressure. I had to be fast *and* accurate, because the people who harvested the fruit were paid according to how many pounds of produce they harvested each day, and there were always those employees who were just sure you were trying to short them. Even an honest mistake was unacceptable, so this might explain why I was always comfortable in math class.

After the rhubarb harvest, the cherries started coming in — sweet cherries first, followed by the tart or pie cherries. Today, cherries are harvested by machines that shake the trees, causing the fruit to fall onto a device wrapped around the bottom of the tree that looks like a very large upside-down umbrella. But when I was a youngster, we climbed ladders up into the tree and picked each cherry by hand, placing them into a bucket that hung over our shoulders on a long strap. I didn't mind going up into the trees at all, but soon my dad had me riding the big truck the fruit pickers would bring their buckets to. As each worker poured his bucket of cherries into a box, I would hand him a ticket that he would turn in at the end of the day for his pay. Obviously, the more buckets credited to him, the more he got paid, so everyone moved pretty fast. In between buckets, I sorted through the recent delivery and tossed out any damaged or overripe fruit. We sold our cherries direct to the cannery, and if they found too many bad cherries when we delivered them, they wouldn't pay us the premium price. It was my job to make sure that never happened.

It was on the back of that truck that I also began my management training, because every now and then a worker would bring his bucket to me, and I would notice it wasn't quite filled up. Technically, I wasn't a supervisor or boss, but I was responsible for making sure none of the workers tried to short us. So if a bucket came in that could hold another half pound of cherries, I had to send the worker back, which meant lost time on his part as he climbed off the truck, walked back to his tree, climbed the ladder, and picked more cherries.

Our farm hired all kinds of people to work the fields. Some were men who had lost their jobs and needed some income while they looked for another job. Others were migrant workers who depended on farms like ours for employment. And we also hired a lot of high school kids, giving them an opportunity to earn some spending money.

By the time I was in high school, my role at the farm became more supervisory, so I had to learn how to be a good boss to some of my best friends from high school. It wasn't easy. Because I was so loyal to my dad—and because I knew we depended solely on the farm for our own survival—I took my responsibilities seriously. I knew how hard he worked, and that he expected no less of me. So if I saw a group of my friends sitting around and talking when they were supposed to be working, I tried to get them back on task without making them mad at me. Most of the time I think they understood that I was just doing my job, but sometimes it was clear they weren't all that pleased having to take orders from me.

During the peach harvest, we opened the fruit stand—usually in July—and that's when I would shift from working in the fields to the retail environment of selling directly to our customers. This was back when people canned their own fruits and vegetables, so it wasn't unusual for customers to buy their produce in large quantities. As the season progressed, we would add tomatoes, cucumbers, different varieties of peaches, and finally the apples. At least that was how it was supposed to work out. Unfortunately, we had no control over the weather.

Weather Worries

If you're a farmer, you're always worried about too much rain or too little. There were some years when the majority of our crops were wiped out by bad weather, and we had nothing to sell. Nothing. But because so many people in the area depended on us, my dad would buy produce from other areas of the state and bring it to our stand just so we could serve our customers. During those years, we lost money, so as a family we had to tighten our belts and do without some things for the rest of the year, hoping the next season would be better.

I remember as a kid, though, being torn between the challenges of the weather and the fun that came with it. For example, in April my brothers and sister and I actually loved hearing frost warnings on the radio, because it meant we got to stay up all night to keep the smudge pots lit. Smudge pots are sort of like big kerosene lanterns whose heat protects the trees in our orchards. Or at least they're supposed to. But to us kids, it meant we could skip school the next day and not get punished, because the schools in rural areas made allowances for kids from farm families. It wasn't until I got a little older that I understood what was fun for us was stressful for my dad and grandfather. If we didn't keep the pots lit — or if the temperature was so low that the heat from the pots wasn't enough to fight off the frost — we would lose the entire year's crop.

If we got through the cooler spring weather unscathed, we still had weather worries. As much as we needed rain to make everything grow, if it came at the wrong time, it could create another disaster. Consider our cherry crop. Cherries need rain to grow big and juicy. But if we got a good rain just before harvest and it was followed by a hot, sunny day, the skins of the cherries split, making them useless to the customer. With our peaches, we needed just the right amount of rain. Too little and the fruit would be small. Too much and the peaches would fall to the ground and could then only be sold for a much lower price. And that's just how it seemed to go all the way up to the final harvest of our apples. Disaster loomed behind every cloud.

You would think all that stress would cause a lot of anxiety for my dad and grandfather, but they were very even-tempered and took things in stride. In fact, I only saw my dad lose his cool once, and it had nothing to do with the weather or lost crops. One day while I was working at the fruit stand, I was selling some peaches to a customer who accused me of cheating him. All fruit is graded according to quality, with the highest-quality fruit bringing the highest price. This man accused me of selling him peaches that had been picked up off the ground (the lowest grade) and trying to pass them off as the top grade. What had actually happened is that the peaches he was considering purchasing had gotten some dust on them from the road that ran in front of the field, and he took that as a sign that these were from the ground. The more I tried to explain, the angrier he got. My dad was at the fruit stand at the time, and when he heard this man accuse me of lying and saw me break down in tears, he walked over and ordered the man to leave the fruit stand and never come back.

Little Farm Girl from Oregon

Aside from the constant threat of weather-related disasters and the hot, hard work in the fields, life was pretty good for this little farm girl from rural Oregon. I attended a little four-room schoolhouse from the first through the eighth grades. I loved that school. It was as though we were all just one big happy family. I really liked my teachers, but two teachers in particular instilled in me the notion that I could always do better. They were really tough, and even though I got good grades, that didn't mean much to them. They pushed me to do my best, regardless of what grade I got. I have so much respect for teachers. When you ask people the top five people who influenced their lives, typically two teachers are mentioned.

Ironically, even though I went to a little rural school, it was there I learned that gender didn't have to be a limitation. For whatever reason, when it was time for recess, I never wanted to join the girls who skipped rope or played hopscotch. Instead, I was always with the boys playing football, baseball, or basketball, and no one seemed to mind. No one ever told me a girl couldn't play shortstop, and so when the bell rang for recess, I ran out to the baseball field and took my place between second and third base. And to their credit, the boys never treated me like a "token" girl integrating their sport. If I covered second base on a potential double play, the guy running from first would do his best to take me out, but just as he would do to one of the guys.

Life Lessons

During those seventeen or eighteen years of growing up on the farm, I never once thought of it as career training. But as I look back on those experiences, it's clear they helped prepare me for what I do today as a business leader. For example, I spend a lot of time working on budgets and putting together complex deals. I know that some of my colleagues dread "working the numbers," but having had to subtract the weight of those boxes from the overall weight of the produce conditioned me to not be afraid of anything related to math.

I learned before I was sixteen not only what it was like having to motivate and even hold employees accountable, but to also do it in a way that preserved their dignity and even encouraged them to try harder and become better workers. Talk about an important lesson for a leader in today's business environment. Likewise, I had to be prepared for anything, because on the farm, anything could happen, and you couldn't convene a meeting to figure out what to do next.

Once when I was sixteen, I led a crew of about fifty people during the peach harvest. They ranged in age from about sixteen to fifty, and everything was going smoothly until a gentleman fell off his ladder and began going into convulsions on the ground. I'd had no first-aid training, but I remembered my parents talking about epileptic seizures and how important it is to keep a person from swallowing his tongue. I had no idea whether this was epilepsy, but I tore off a section of a tree branch and stuck it in his mouth to keep his tongue from slipping down into his throat. It turned out he was okay—he had actually suffered a drug overdose—but experiences like these taught me at a young age to be ready for anything and not to panic when the unexpected happens.

Largely due to the influence of my parents, I learned from a very early age the value of self-discipline. *Learned* may not even be the right word, because I just sort of *absorbed* a disciplined life. On the farm, I really had no choice. When it was time to thin the fruit trees, I had to climb the ladder and pull off the extra fuzzy peaches just so. It didn't matter if I felt like doing it or not, and in the hot weather the fuzz got really itchy on my skin. But to put it off could mean a smaller yield, which meant we might not be able to pay all our bills. And as each crop ripened, we had to pick them right then or end up with spoiled produce that no one would buy. Trust me, you won't get very far in any career without a healthy dose of self-discipline. When you're a leader, no one comes around and reminds you to get the job done. The world of commercial real estate is demanding—as I'm sure your line of work is. When I'm on a deadline to complete a major project, I've never had a problem sticking with it until it's done, and I credit those long hours in the fields.

Perhaps most important, I grew up believing that I could do or be anything I wanted. Neither my parents nor the community surrounding me could be considered progressive, and I don't think I heard the word *feminist* until I got to college. But not once did my parents or teachers or friends lead me to believe I couldn't do something just because I was a poor farm girl. Thankfully, my dad was wise enough not to assign me to a crew of rowdy guys who would be all alone with me out in the middle of an orchard. But aside from that, he expected me to work as hard and as long as any guy on the farm.

Growing up on the farm also planted a seed of desire inside me to live the balanced life I saw my parents live. Their lives revolved around three things that have become so important to me today: faith, family, and work. For them, it was natural—they did not deliberately work at balancing these areas that I now have to work so hard to manage. My dad's career was the farm, and my mom's career was taking care of all of us, including our home. Fortunately for us kids, work was a family affair, so I never experienced having my dad or mom miss events in my life because of work. They were always there, which probably influenced me to try and figure out ways to be there for my own kids.

My family also had nonwork time doing things together. My mom was a great cook, and we always shared at least one meal a day around the dining room table. And we always went to church except in the summer in the middle of our busy season. In fact, other than school, church pretty much rounded out my social life, because a lot of my cousins and friends went to the same little country church. Unlike a lot of young people, I never fussed about going to church, because I knew I would be with my friends (and I knew it wouldn't do any good anyway). And when I hit my teenage years, I benefited from a great youth group that made going to church something I looked forward to.

What's *Your* Story?

I realize everyone has a different story, but as we explore the challenges of balancing the things that are important to us as professional Christian women, I'd like you to take some time to reflect on your own early years. They don't have to be as idyllic as mine might seem, for even things that are unpleasant in our past can influence us for the better.

For example, because I grew up in a rural environment, I found myself busy from the time I woke up until late at night when I went to bed. I was usually the first one in my family to get up in the morning, and I would go out to the barn and feed my 4-H cow and horse and clean their stalls. Then I would head back into the house and practice the piano as everyone else was getting up. Then it was off to school, followed by sports after school, then homework, and then I sewed my clothes until late at night. No TV, just plenty of wholesome things to keep me busy.

The downside of all this is that it conditioned me to go full speed all the time, and there have been times when this personality trait of mine has gotten in the way of my relationships—to say nothing of my own well-being. Once I realized that this wasn't so much a flaw as it was the product of my childhood, I was able to address my busyness and learn that it's okay to relax—to shut down from time to time and experience the benefits of quiet reflection.

So what about you? How have your earliest experiences shaped you into the person you are today? What strengths do you bring from your childhood and teenage years that you can build on, and what weaknesses do you need to address? Like it or not, we are the products of our past experiences and relationships. How you approach the challenges of your work and personal life has been strongly influenced by your parents, your teachers, and your friends. Take some time to reflect on those experiences today.

For Reflection or Discussion

1. Who were the people that influenced you the most during your childhood and youth?

2. Either by example or through their direct teaching, what did you learn from these people? How exactly did they influence you?

3. What events or experiences in your childhood and youth do you feel had a positive influence on you? A negative influence? Explain.

4. What are you doing to build on those positive experiences? How have they helped you in your career?

5. What are you doing to overcome the negative influences from your past? How are you keeping them from interfering with your success at work or at home?

6. Are there younger people in your life who may be watching and learning from you? If so, what are they learning?

7. What gets you excited? Does your work take advantage of the things you naturally loved to do as you grew up?

Rough Start

Even if your early years weren't all that rosy, they can still have a positive influence on you. Just ask Erin Botsford. When Erin was eleven, her father died, leaving her mother and five siblings with an insurance policy that barely paid for the funeral. "We had nothing," Erin recalls. "No money for college, weddings, new clothes. Nothing!"

When she turned sixteen, things got worse. Driving home one day, she was involved in an accident that caused a fatality, and she was charged with manslaughter. "Our lawyer knew we were poor and told my mom that if I pleaded guilty he wouldn't charge us anything for handling the case. When my mom told me to plead guilty, I told her I couldn't because I hadn't done anything wrong. I'll never forget her words: 'Honey, we have no choice, because we don't have any money.'"

Still, Erin refused to plead guilty. "I determined then and there that I would *never* allow myself to be in such a helpless position again," she explains.

Her mother took out a second mortgage to pay for Erin's defense, which eventually cleared her of all charges. But Erin vowed to pay every penny of that mortgage back. "For the next ten years that bill came every month, and with each check I wrote I put that terrible memory further behind me."

Erin also began to make good on her promise to herself to get out of poverty. An honor student throughout high school, she was elected junior class president, then during her senior year, she worked an eight-hour shift after school every day at a local hospital. Her hard work in school earned her a full scholarship, but she left college after one quarter because she couldn't afford her living expenses and still pay back her mother. She moved back in with her mom and enrolled in a nearby college while she worked the graveyard shift stocking shelves at a grocery store to pay for tuition, to continue paying back her mom, and to try to save a little for the future.

By the time she was in her twenties, she had saved $20,000. After putting a $3,000 down payment on a townhome, she invested the rest in what she hoped would become her retirement. But thanks to an unscrupulous investor, she lost every penny and had to start over again. That could have been the knock-out punch, but today Erin owns her own company, is happily married to a commercial airline pilot, and was named one of the "Top 100 Women Financial Advisers" in *Barron's* magazine.

How has this successful mom, wife, and business owner turned an unpleasant past into a positive influence?

"Discipline and attitude," she explains. "I learned from my childhood that I'm responsible for my attitude. Every morning I am given the gift of a brand new day, and it's my choice what to do with it, regardless of the circumstances."

As a busy mom married to a military pilot, who after retirement became a commercial pilot, she had to learn how to juggle her many responsibilities. "We moved seventeen times in fourteen years, but I've never missed a single event in my son's life. It's all about keeping your priorities straight. We might *say* family comes first, but what does your calendar say?"

She applied that same discipline to her marriage. "From the very beginning, every Friday night was date night, and after eight every night is Mommy and Daddy time. Our son knew we cared about him because we adjusted our schedules to be with him, but he also saw that we took time for each other too."

Whether your past is a fairy tale or a horror story, only *you* can determine how it will play out—as a tragedy, or as a feel-good story with a happy ending.

from harrisburg
to harvard

WHAT DID YOU LEARN IN COLLEGE? Do you ever find yourself thinking that those required courses didn't do all that much to prepare you for the job you're doing right now? You'd be surprised just how much your college years help shape your career. College is more than an education—it's an experience. For me, it was an experience that began to uncover some hidden qualities that helped take me to where I am today, and if you look back at your own experience, you'll likely find the same is true for you.

As the crow flies, our farm in Harrisburg was only about forty miles from Oregon State University in Corvallis. But for this little farm girl, it may as well have been a thousand miles away. By anyone else's standards, Corvallis barely qualified as a small city with its 45,000 residents, but to me, it was like another world. The university population alone was about ten times bigger than my hometown, and with every mile northward we drove on Peoria Road on that first trip to the campus, my heart seemed to beat faster with a mixture of fear and anticipation.

Even though I was a small-town girl, I couldn't wait to get to college, and I jumped right into the campus scene from the minute my mom dropped me off at my dorm. I immediately got involved in student activities, joined a sorority, and of course cheered like crazy in the student section of the football stadium on Saturday afternoons, especially when those lowly Ducks from the rival University of Oregon waddled into town.

But unlike a lot of small-town girls who get to the big university campus, I somehow avoided the party-till-you-drop scene that usually results in a lot of freshmen dropping out after one semester. I'd like to take credit for being so disciplined, but my good behavior was largely the result of three things: my faith, a desire to do my best with my God-given gifts, and a hefty school bill that I paid as much as possible with academic scholarships.

Unfortunately, I got my roommate by the potluck method, and by the end of my first week of dorm life, I knew I was in trouble. Although I could have chosen a roommate like a lot of incoming freshmen did, for some reason I let the housing people do it for me. Usually they do a great job of matching people up, but in my case, they blew it. Actually, I don't blame anyone, but I think you'd have to look real hard to find two people in the world who were as different and incompatible as my roommate and me. I was focused on school, and she liked to party. I was an early bird, and she was a night owl. By this time, at the ripe old age of eighteen, I thought I had learned how to get along with all types of people after working alongside the other workers on the farm, so I was pretty sure our problems weren't *my* fault. But my roommate probably felt the same way about me. The university had a process for changing roommates, but one of the things I learned on the farm is that you finish whatever you start, so I wasn't about to become a quitter. I was determined to at least get through one semester with her, even if it killed both of us.

However, my disciplined style worked well with her schedule, since we were so opposite. I would get up early before she did and go study in the library before my classes. Then when my classes were done for the day, I'd go back to the library and stay there until it closed. I practically lived in the library that first semester. I was so focused on my studies that I became one of those rare freshmen to pull a 4.0 grade-point average my first year in college.

But it was my desire to do well that kept me from getting caught up in the party scene. My parents' farm provided us with a comfortable standard of living, but there wasn't enough left over to pay for college. And because they owned so much land, on paper they came off as being too wealthy to qualify me for any state aid. In other words, if any of us kids wanted to go to college, we had to find a way to pay for it, and I learned early on that there were two ways I could do that: get good grades in high school so that I might get an academic scholarship to help pay for college, and save as much money as I could from working on the farm. When it's your own hard work and hard-earned money paying your school bill, you think twice about staying out all night and blowing off your classes the next day. To keep the academic scholarship I earned when I graduated from high school, I had to maintain good grades in college, a further incentive to study. I'm not sure they set out to teach me this, but one of the best lessons my parents taught me on the farm was the value of money. It was something you worked hard to get, so you were careful how you spent it.

Growing at the Gathering

What really kept me grounded, however, was my faith. Through being involved in student activities and my sorority, I got to know a group of friends who attended a Bible study I attended called the Gathering. I wasn't sure what to expect when one of my friends invited me to join a group of students who got together to sing and pray and study the Bible. But I went, and the minute I walked through the door, I knew I wasn't in Kansas anymore. I had never seen anything like this. There must have been two hundred college students in this large room just about two blocks off campus—more people than I ever saw in my entire church, even on Easter Sunday!

And the music. Back in my home church, the music on Sundays consisted of a couple of very slow hymns, and that was pretty much it. But here the music was lively and upbeat, accompanied by guitars, with everyone singing as if they really enjoyed it. Never before had I heard anyone stand up and share their faith, but this was probably the best part of the Gathering, as ordinary students just like me spoke easily yet passionately about what God was doing in their lives.

While I was certain that I was a Christian, it was at the Gathering that I began to fully understand the "personal relationship" side of my faith, and I began to really grow and mature as a believer. It was also at the Gathering that I cultivated some dear friendships that are a strong and positive influence on me to this day. One of the keys to success in college and in the workplace is to have good friends who care about you, and that's one of the bonuses I got from the Gathering.

What I really loved about the Gathering, however, was that it taught me how to integrate my faith into my everyday life. Growing up in Harrisburg, my faith was pretty much going to church on Sunday. It was an important compartment in my life, but it stayed in the compartment the rest of the week. I was active in Sunday school and my church's youth group, but never really thought much about my faith when I was working in the fields or playing flag football with the guys. At the Gathering I learned to make faith the center of my life and carry it with me wherever I went.

A New Family

During my freshman year at Oregon State, I joined a sorority and moved into the sorority house my sophomore year. That solved the roommate problem by giving me a "family," complete with big-sister role models and regular family powwows where we addressed problems, planned events, and reviewed our finances. Judy Looseley, the president of our sorority, was one of those women I looked up to who influenced me so much by her example: premed student, smart, strong Christian, athlete. I also loved my big "sis," Kris Stout, who had a beautiful singing voice that she shared at the Gathering. Just being around them made me want to be a better person. It seemed that during my time in college, God had his hand on my life and guided me into these wonderful relationships that nurtured me and are a vital part of my life even today. Many call it networking. I call it keeping in touch with friends who are great people. If you happen to be in college now, or grad school, I can't emphasize enough the importance of developing strong friendships with people who have your best interests in mind.

By this time, I was really active in MUPC, the group charged with the responsibility of planning and executing all the various activities for students. Specifically, I was in charge of three major campuswide events: Homecoming Week, Mom's Weekend, and Dad's Weekend. In some ways, I bit off more than I could chew, because these three events required hours of my time. It was my job to make sure that not only all the students on campus, but thousands of returning alumni and parents as well, had a great time.

Now conventional wisdom would suggest that you can get too extended in college with extracurricular activities, but I'm a big believer that what happens outside the classroom can be just as educational as what happens inside. Maybe even more so. My major in fashion merchandising taught me a lot of valuable technical and theoretical information that I'm sure helped me in some of my jobs, but what I learned just from helping to plan Homecoming Week gave me many of the skills that I use today as a business executive. I had to recruit volunteers and assign them to the right job, execute events, such as the big homecoming parade and yet stay within budget, evaluate the work of my volunteers and show them how to improve, and with everything, meet our deadlines. I eventually was elected president of my sorority, Alpha Chi Omega, Chi chapter, and that further taught me how to cope with the tougher side of leadership. We had sixty girls living in the house, with sixty more living outside, and I had to make sure we all got along, paid our dues, did our assigned housework, and functioned as one big happy family. I learned so much about motivating and inspiring others, and I also learned how hard it was to make difficult decisions with peers.

One semester I kept getting reports of missing jewelry. After checking things out over a six- to eight-month period, I discovered that one of my sorority sisters, a kleptomaniac, was stealing from us. One of the most difficult leadership decisions I have ever made came when I had to call the girl's parents and ask them to come and get her because we could no longer trust her. Another time it came to my attention that one of our sisters was bulimic, but like most who are afflicted with this horrible disease, she didn't want to admit it, and I had to be the one to confront her and try to get her some professional help.

These weren't just my fellow students, but friends. But as I have learned throughout my career, most of the people who report to you also become like friends; yet you still have to make the tough calls. If you aspire to leadership, ask yourself this question: "If one of my friends really messed up on the job, would I be able to confront her and even dismiss her if that was warranted?"

A Chance to Fail

One of the reasons I'm so big on encouraging younger women to get involved in as many extracurricular activities as possible during their college years is that it gives them on-the-job training before they head off into the real world. One of the key leadership-development opportunities for women is to learn how to make crucial decisions and accept the fact that you won't be liked by everyone.

It also gives you a chance to fail.

One year I tried out for the cheerleading team. I was a cheerleader from the fifth grade through my senior year and craved the whole college experience of being able to lead the entire stadium in cheering for the old home team. My best friend, Cindy, was also trying out. When I was in high school, trying out for anything was sort of a formality because I made every team. So I pretty much went into the cheerleading tryouts thinking I had a good shot because I had never really failed at anything before. Well, that was back in little old Harrisburg. I should have known that the best cheerleaders from hundreds of high schools throughout the Northwest and beyond would be trying out, so when they posted the results and my name wasn't on the list, I was devastated. However Cindy had made the squad. I was excited for her. Instead of crying the whole day, I practically ran back to the sorority house and spent the rest of the day cleaning my big sister's room. That helped. The more I worked, the less I felt sorry for myself, and to this day that has become a great coping skill for disappointment.

From London to IBM

If the big city of Corvallis opened my window to a bigger world than existed in Harrisburg, spending a semester as an exchange student at the University of London was like blowing the roof off my world. I scraped together enough money for plane fare and lived with a family who became my British "mum and dad." I bought a Eurail Pass so that I could travel on the cheap on free weekends. For someone who had hardly been out of the state of Oregon, navigating the "tube," finding hostels in France and Italy, and hitchhiking with one other girl and two guys contributed to a growing awareness that I could do anything. It also taught me that despite cultural, language, and even religious differences, people are pretty much the same the world over.

A few weeks before leaving for London, two of my best friends—John Stirek and Dan Boyden—were talking with me about my future plans. I was majoring in fashion merchandising and had worked during the summer, Christmas, and spring breaks in various jobs related to this industry. And I hated it. I realized, almost in a panic, that I was getting a major in something I didn't want to do. But I didn't want to change my major because it would mean at least an extra year of college expenses. So Dan said, "Why don't you apply for an MBA at Harvard?" He had applied on a "deferred admit" program where you worked for two years right out of college before you went on to Harvard. I was certain I wouldn't get accepted because I wasn't a business major, but Dan persisted.

"Look, they're going to look at all your extracurricular experiences here and your good grades and decide you're just the type of person they're looking for. So just take a bunch of business classes your senior year to get a minor in business."

It sort of made sense to me, so the day before I got on the plane for London, I typed up the application, put it in an envelope, and handed it to my parents, asking them to drop it in the mail for me.

"What is it?" my mom asked.

"It's my application for an MBA program at Harvard," I proudly answered.

"What's an MBA?" my dad asked.

"Where's Harvard?" my mom chipped in.

I got accepted into the program, which meant I needed to find a job that would support me for two years before I went to Harvard Business School. Being a major university, we always had recruiters on campus from all sorts of businesses, but I quickly discovered that not too many were interested in hiring someone who would be leaving in two years. My British "dad" worked for IBM in London and once was kind enough to take me to their headquarters to show me around. I have to admit I was really impressed with what I saw, so when I learned that IBM would have a representative on campus, I signed up for an appointment. It turned out that they loved the idea of hiring someone on a deferred admission to Harvard Business School, and in fact, this dear recruiter recommended that I be sent to a division headquartered in a town close to Princeton, New Jersey, so that I could get the kind of experience that would be helpful in my MBA program.

So right after I graduated from Oregon State, my dad and I left for Princeton, where we put a deposit on an apartment, found a hotel where I could stay until my apartment was available, and bought a car. The people at IBM had offered me a relocation package, but I told them I would be cheap since I had only two cartons of clothes and an air mattress that I used for a bed until I got my first paycheck and bought a real one.

Right out of the blocks, I was assigned to work with two IBM veterans, and together we created IBM Direct, the company's first effort to sell their products through catalogs and the mail. Talk about a great experience for someone right out of college. IBM was—and is—a huge global company, and at the time was not considered particularly open to change. They had always relied on their world-class sales force, so getting them to accept a new way of selling required a lot of careful negotiation and vision casting. Of course, I was the new kid on the block and spent most of my time observing, but it taught me a lot about how to bring people around to a different point of view. It also continued to open new windows for me, as once a week I would take the train into Manhattan to meet with our ad agency in what is now the Trump Tower.

I might have gotten caught up in all the glitz and glamour of this part of my job, except for two things, my focus on my faith and a desire to have a family. My spiritual growth during college had given me a higher perspective from which to evaluate the trappings of success. I definitely enjoyed being part of an exciting team working in New Jersey and Manhattan, but it was just as easy to go back to my little apartment because I knew I did not need any of that in order to be happy. It was also around this time that I got my first performance review, and it too brought me down to earth because it wasn't the A plus I had gotten used to. I learned that there were areas of my professional life that needed some work, and that instilled in me an even greater desire to focus on what really mattered. At first it stung a little, even though my supervisor did a great job of affirming other areas of my performance. But after I got over the initial hurt feelings, I realized he was right on target with his criticism and was doing me a favor by bringing it to my attention.

Throughout my career, I've had all sorts of evaluations and reviews, from 360-degree reviews (where you are reviewed by your peers and colleagues) to professional assessments from outside sources to eventually maybe the toughest review of all: a lengthy and very thorough self-evaluation of every area of my life as part of my MBA program at Harvard. I can honestly say I learned something valuable from each one. You too will experience various reviews and assessments, and sometimes the tendency is to just go through the motions or, worse, ignore the "needs improvement" categories. Yet those reviews are a great way to grow and become a more valuable employee. The key is to be open to criticism rather than fight it. To listen to it rather than get defensive about it. Yes, it might not feel very good to have someone point out shortcomings in your work, but how are you going to get better if you're unaware of those shortcomings? How can you expect to improve if you don't know what to work on?

Life at Harvard

My two years at IBM were a whirlwind of new discoveries about the business world, and by the end, I knew that this was what I wanted to do. I enjoyed managing people around a common goal that helped grow the business. In fact, if you're thinking of going from college into an advanced degree program, I would highly recommend getting some work experience just to make sure you're a good fit with the kind of work you *think* you want to do. By the time I got to Harvard, I had a better idea of who I was as a person and what the business world was like, which helped a lot, because trust me, as I set foot on that hallowed campus, all I could think was, "What am I doing here?" I was certain everyone else I saw was so much smarter than I was, and the intimidation factor of Harvard just sort of loomed over me.

Once again, I was assigned a roommate potluck, only this time she was fantastic. She made me feel like I was right where I was supposed to be, and to this day Jill Perrin is one of my close friends. I also found a group of good friends at the HBS Christian Fellowship.

I worked hard and felt like I was doing a pretty good job. Then at the end of the semester, the envelope with my grades appeared in my mailbox. I nervously opened it, and my eyes skipped over the good grades and landed on my grade for Organizational Behavior. At Harvard, if you failed a class, they called it "looping." I had just looped my first class! The first failure in my entire academic life! Fortunately Jill was in the room; otherwise I'm not sure what I would have done.

"Oh, that's nothing," she laughed. "We've all looped at least one class. The first one's always the hardest. It happens."

I guess I just needed to hear that it was okay to fail. I'd been pretty successful my entire academic life and had never even considered what it would be like to get anything less than an A in a class. Jill helped me realize I was human, just like everyone else in the program. She even had me laughing about it for a while, but I did cry myself to sleep that night.

Eventually I realized that failing at something didn't make me a failure, and that no matter how hard you fall, you can always pick yourself up, dust off the damage, and get right back in the game. Which is exactly what I did. Again, I was paying my own way, and my total expenses for one year at Harvard were four times higher than Oregon State. I wasn't about to let this one failed class stand in the way of finishing the program. Ultimately, I ended up in the top 10 percent of my class at graduation.

Continuing Your Education

Do you need to go immediately from college to Harvard Business School to be successful? Of course not. I have many friends who are in leadership positions who never went beyond a bachelor's degree. And while the words *Harvard* or *Stanford* may initially get recruiters' attention, I know from my own experience of hiring people that it takes more than good grades or a brand-name school to land a job. In fact, I'm less likely to hire someone with a four point from a prestigious school if I don't see evidence in her resume of some extracurricular that required leadership skills and other real-life experiences. I honestly think my heavy involvement in campus activities at Oregon State plus my work experience right out of college were as big a plus for me as my Harvard graduate degree.

At the same time, I would strongly urge you to consider continuing your education beyond your undergraduate degree, especially if you have your sights set on an executive-level position. Today's work environment is much more competitive than it was when I was starting out, so having an advanced degree could be the edge you need to move up to the next level. An added benefit is the wider network that comes with graduate school. The good news is that you don't have to quit your job to go back to school. Universities often offer classes in the evening or on weekends that allow you to pursue an advanced degree without leaving your job. And many companies provide tuition assistance that will enable you to take courses while you continue working for them. That's a benefit you really can't ignore.

Finally, you may need to look at your current skill sets in relation to the potential changes in your particular profession. Have you stayed current with those changes, or do you need to consider taking additional courses or training to make sure you don't get left behind? For example, I recently learned of a talented marketing executive who was replaced because he had not kept pace with the way the digital world had impacted his profession. The world is changing so rapidly that you really ought to think of education as a lifelong journey. Fortunately, it's easier now than it ever has been to continue your education, and it has the added advantage of expanding your own network.

I left Harrisburg with high hopes, a foundation of strong values, and a determination to do my very best. My experiences in and out of the classroom at Oregon State and then at Harvard began to mold me into the person I am today. Most important, those years of writing papers and taking exams taught me that even a small-town farm girl can do things she never dreamed were possible.

For Reflection or Discussion

1. Identify at least three positive influences from your undergraduate or graduate experience that helped shape you into the person you are today.

2. What was your most difficult challenge in college, and how did it affect your experience there?

3. Identify at least one thing you learned from a class that you have been able to apply to your current position. Identify at least one thing you learned from an extracurricular activity or other non-academic activity that you have been able to apply to your current position.

4. What advice would you give a young woman entering college today? Why?

5. What role did faith or spirituality play in your life prior to college? Did it change when you left home for college? Explain.

6. Identify at least two things you learned about yourself during your college experience.

7. How do you network? Do you keep in touch with people you naturally want to keep in touch with forever? Who are the people in your life that share your focus on faith, family, and profession and know you very well?

Should You Go Back to School?

In most professions, you won't get your foot in the door without a bachelor's degree. But what about further education? Do you need an advanced degree to move up in the company? Will you earn more money if you get your master's degree?

According to a 2008 U.S. Census Bureau survey of people 25 years old and older, the median income for a bachelor's-degree holder was $47,853. That number jumped to $63,174 for those with a graduate or professional degree.[1] Over the course of a career, that could mean anywhere from $350,000 to $400,000 more in earnings for those with an advanced degree.

On the other hand, that advanced degree requires investments of time and money. Tuition for an advanced degree ranges from $5,000 to $30,000 a year. Will you take out a loan or pay as you go? Does your company offer tuition assistance? Should you ask for a leave of absence or take classes in the evening and on weekends?

If you're considering going back to school, discuss the potential impact it will have on your job with someone in your HR department. It's also a good idea to check with others in your company who have earned an advanced degree. Finally, Kiplinger — publishers of helpful business and finance information — offers a free resource at their website that will help you determine how an advanced degree will impact you financially. You can access this resource at www .kiplinger.com/tools/managing/college/gradschool.html.

reality sets in

I GOT MARRIED.

It sort of started back at Oregon State. Maybe you can relate, but as I approached my senior year, I just began feeling as if I needed to start thinking about marriage. I had always enjoyed dating guys—even back in high school. In college, I even had a fairly serious relationship with a guy who asked me to marry him. I liked the guy a lot and enjoyed being with him. I might even have accepted his proposal except for one thing. We had spent countless hours talking about faith, and he totally rejected my beliefs, so I knew he wasn't the one for me. But that didn't mean I didn't want to find Mr. Right. I wouldn't call it panic, but I saw many of my friends and sorority sisters getting engaged and began wondering if I would ever meet someone with whom I could live the rest of my life. It didn't help that just about everyone began asking me when I was going to get engaged. Here I was barely twenty-two, and well-meaning people were saying things like, "You know, you're not getting any younger." It seemed like America's favorite pastime was playing cupid to anyone who didn't have her Mrs. degree right after she got her BA.

At the same time, I knew I wanted to pursue a career, and with the IBM job to look forward to, it's not as if I was ready to put all that on hold and start stalking a husband. And to be perfectly honest, there really was no one on the horizon at the time. So with the excitement of a new job right around the corner, my desire for romance and marriage just sort of fell onto the back burner. In fact, marriage was the last thing I was thinking about after I graduated from Oregon State and returned home to get ready for my big move to New Jersey.

Besides, the whole dating scene gets a little complicated once you're out of college. Instead of a campus full of guys to choose from, you're stuck in an office where you might find an eligible candidate, but office romances create their own set of dynamics and might even be frowned upon by management. So that leaves you with few options to meet people who share your values. Happy hour with a group of friends from work? Possibly, but just don't get so "happy" that you can't tell the difference between a good guy and a jerk. Internet dating? It's okay, as long as you realize that a person can be anything he wants to be in cyberspace (see sidebar on page 63). Speed dating? This relatively new phenomenon provides a structure for meeting a lot of guys in a short time, but it also seems a little hectic to me. Why rush a good thing? Blind dates? If it's set up by a good friend who knows you well, why not? If arranged by someone from work you barely know, not! Singles groups? Obviously a great opportunity to meet other singles, but it could identify you as being a little desperate. Special interest groups? Excellent—if you belong to a health club or are in a reading group, you at least know the guys there share an interest with you.

Which brings me to how I met my husband, along with a particular bias I have regarding a good place to meet guys who *may* be compatible with you. Four years of college had left me broke, yet I wanted a little adventure with my sister before I left home for good. We had always been close, and I so looked forward to one last special time with her alone. But since neither of us had any money, our big trip would have to be done on the cheap. We had a cousin who lived in Oklahoma, and when we called to ask if he could put us up in his bachelor pad for a few days, he readily agreed. Okay, Oklahoma wasn't exactly the French Riviera, but it did have the one thing we craved, being from Oregon: sunshine. And it wouldn't cost us much. So off we went to Oklahoma City, where we enjoyed the sun during the day while our cousin worked, and then hung out with him in the evening. Sunday came, and just like back home, we got up and went to church, and that's where I met Stan.

I'm not going to say we were made for each other, but it was pretty clear from the start that Stan and I had a lot in common. He came from a big, supportive family, just like I did, so I knew family was important to him. He owned his own business, so we both shared an interest in terms of our careers. As we dated and got to know each other, I knew that like me, he hoped to have his own family someday. And most important, we shared a strong faith in God. In fact, our priorities lined up perfectly: faith, family, career, in that order.

Okay, he was pretty easy on the eyes too.

I'm not saying that church is the only place to meet guys, but it's not a bad place to start. To be honest, I didn't go to church that day to meet a guy, but had I skipped that Sunday, I wouldn't have met Stan.

Long-Distance Romance

The only slight challenge was that Stan lived in Tulsa, Oklahoma, and when I met him, I was just a few days from moving to New Jersey to start my new job at IBM. After that, I had two years of Harvard ahead of me. By the time my sister and I headed back to Oregon, it was clear to me that Stan was someone special. I knew that long-distance relationships didn't always last, but at the time it seemed that so many things were falling into place, this just might be the guy. Task-oriented by nature, I was now able to check off all the important goals in my life: college graduate? Check! Good job? Check! Good MBA program? Check! And finally, potential husband? Check!

Over the next several months, we burned up the phone lines and exchanged numerous letters (hard to believe, but this was before email and texting). The more we talked, the more I felt myself falling in love with him, and I was pretty sure Stan felt the same way about me. He had a great sense of humor and a tenderness about him that truly captured my heart. We connected on so many levels, and the few times we were together in person only further convinced me that this just might be the man I would marry. Sure enough, Stan asked me to marry him, and in the summer of 1984, we got married.

That was the easy part.

An Unconventional Beginning

Stan and I both knew it would be difficult to begin our marriage more than a thousand miles apart, but he respected my desire to finish my MBA, and I wasn't about to ask him to move to Massachusetts. In fact, one of the things that I think attracted us to each other was mutual respect. I suppose he could have been intimidated by a woman so determined to earn an MBA from Harvard, but he was totally supportive of my plans and encouraged me to stick with them. And I knew how hard he worked to start a landscape business in Tulsa that was doing well. I figured if he would allow me to finish up my degree even though it meant we would be separated for several months, I would gladly move to Tulsa and begin my career there.

Which is exactly what I did, though not without some raised eyebrows from my classmates. As we neared the end of the program, we were all getting attractive offers from some of the top companies in the world. I'm talking Fortune 500 businesses recruiting us with great positions and the accompanying dizzying salaries and benefits. One of the companies that offered me a position was Trammell Crow, one of the larger commercial real-estate companies in the United States. It was tempting because they had an office in Tulsa, but I didn't think I was cut out for real estate, so I turned them down. So when word got out that I was heading to Oklahoma with no real job offer in hand, the responses ranged from a polite "Oh, that's interesting" to "Tulsa? Are you crazy?"

One of the things I've learned over the years is that not everyone thinks the way I do, especially when it comes to family. When I explained to my Harvard buddies that I was moving to Tulsa because that's where my husband lived and ran his business, they just didn't get it. And even as I moved on and up in the corporate world, I ran into many colleagues who thought there was something wrong with me because my career wasn't the driving force in my life. If you have convictions that cut against the grain of your work world, be prepared to have them challenged. But I've also learned that if you consistently hold on to those convictions and take the time to explain the reasons behind them, you will gain the respect of your colleagues, even if they never fully agree with you.

I'll have to admit there were times when I wondered if maybe I was missing out on greater opportunities by moving to Tulsa. Strange as this may seem, I did not have a career path mapped out for myself, but I knew the value of an MBA from Harvard and that I could be making more money and maybe sign on with a company that would be a better fit for me. I quickly found work as a consultant with a Tulsa-based company, but it wasn't long before I felt as if I was just going through the motions. It wasn't much of a challenge, and it did sort of feed that nagging thought in the back of my head that I should be engaged in something bigger, something more significant.

One of my clients was a major player in the health-care industry, and after working with them for a while they offered me a senior position as chief marketing officer. I eagerly accepted, and I learned a lot. It was my first real management job. However, it lacked a pay-for-performance culture and that was important to me, driven into me since I was little working on the farm. I began to wonder if my friends were right—maybe I *was* spinning my wheels and wasting a very marketable degree.

But at the end of the day, I knew what was most important to me. I loved being a wife and knew that putting my marriage ahead of my job was the right thing to do. After being separated for four years since we first met, except for the summers of 1983 and 1984, it was great to be together full-time. Even though I wasn't exactly where I wanted to be professionally, I was in a good place overall and decided to leave the career in God's hands and enjoy being a wife while forging ahead in health care.

Three Good People

During this time I kept in touch with my two friends from Oregon State, John and Dan. Ironically, they had both gone to work for Trammell Crow after getting their Harvard MBAs. Hearing of my frustration in finding just the right fit for me professionally, they began urging me to reconsider that offer I got from their company while I was still at Harvard. I resisted at first, reminding them that I didn't know that much about commercial real estate, and I wasn't sure it was the type of work that would challenge me. But they persisted, insisting that I would find the company to be a great fit.

Here's where it gets interesting. For some reason, I had kept in touch with George Lippe, the gentleman from Trammell Crow who had recruited me at Harvard. I liked him, and even though I didn't think I was cut out for real estate, I thought he was an impressive guy. I began to think that what really makes a company is the people who are part of it, and here were three people I really liked and respected, and they all worked for the same company. Was God trying to tell me something? If he was, I thought, maybe I should listen.

George called me one day and told me that the company had just bought another major real-estate business, which would triple the size of the business in Tulsa. "If you're going to come, Diane, now's the time."

As a young woman growing in her faith, I prayed about my work and my desire to find a company that would allow me to grow professionally without sacrificing the things that were most important to me. I have come to realize that God speaks to us in many ways, and often he uses other people to assist him. John and Dan were both strong Christians who knew me well, knew my values as well as my strengths and weaknesses. And George's timing could not have been better. It was God's timing. Whenever you face a decision about a new job, pay attention to the people in your life who care deeply about you and who know what's important to you. I truly believe that God directed my steps by using these three men to nudge me in the right direction.

I took the job.

Following God's Leading

Actually, it was more than a job. It turned into a twenty-year and six-month run that exceeded every expectation I could ever have had, which underscores one of the truths from God's Word that has always guided me: "Trust in the LORD with all your heart and lean not on your own understanding; in all your ways acknowledge him, and he will make your paths straight" (Proverbs 3:5–6). Had I listened only to my own understanding, which told me that I wouldn't enjoy working in real estate, I'm not sure how my career would have progressed. By listening to godly counsel from others, I finally landed at a place that exceeded my dreams. That seems to be the way God works, if we just let him.

Almost from my first day on the job at Trammell Crow, I began to feel as if my skills and education were being put to good use. Not only was I hitting my stride in my professional life, but my career fit well with thinking about a family. At this point I didn't have to travel very much out of town. After being separated for almost the first year of our marriage, it was great to spend time together on weekends and focus on our church family, friends, and Oklahoma State games. As you might guess, it wasn't long before I was able to put Trammell Crow to the test in terms of accommodating my commitment to family: I became pregnant with our first child, Christian.

Not only did they accommodate this new development, but they supported it by giving me the flexibility to be a mom and a wife and still grow within the company. And they did it all over again a few years later when our second child, Annie, was born.

If you had looked down on our little family from atop a high building in Tulsa, you would have seen the picture of perfection. Two parents earning plenty of money. Two careers. Two darling children who brought so much joy into our lives. This was exactly what I had dreamed of since I was a little girl. I knew I wanted to be a wife and a mom, but I also knew I wanted to pursue a career, and here I was doing it. And on top of everything, we were part of a church family that nurtured our faith and began to introduce our children to God.

What more could any woman ask for?

For Reflection or Discussion

1. Are you feeling pressure to find a husband? How do you deal with that expectation?
2. If you are married, are you and your husband discussing how to meet both of your goals for faith, family, and career?
3. Is your career and place of work nurturing your life goals? If not, what are you doing to address that situation? Have you included prayer in making your daily decisions?
4. Do you feel pressure from others to focus on your career first? Do you feel you need to gain the approval of others? If so, why?

Young and Single and Then?

It's one thing to be young and single, but what's it like to be single in your forties? According to Stacy, it can be exhausting. A financial consultant and investment banker, Stacy felt more pressure right out of college to pursue her career than to find the right man.

"On the one hand, we were influenced by the feminist movement that told us to focus on our careers first, and at some point a good man would follow. On the other hand, I had just finished getting an expensive college education and felt I needed to put it to good use by starting my career. I also think women my age saw their mothers give up careers, and we knew we wanted more than to just be a stay-at-home mom."

Fresh out of college with a good job, lots of world travel, and plenty of men her age to date, Stacy enjoyed the freedom of being single and getting established in her career. After several years of working and then obtaining her master's degree, she was ready to think more seriously about marriage but discovered it wasn't going to be that easy.

"The pool of eligible men got smaller the further away I got from college," Stacy reports.

Stacy, who is in her early forties, found that not only were there fewer men to choose from, but many were intimidated by a professional woman who had a better job and earned more money than they did. Plus, the whole routine of meeting someone and getting to know them only to discover a red flag, took a lot of time and emotional energy. She tried internet dating but found that to be a mixed blessing.

"The internet allows you to learn a lot more about a person than you would if you met them in person, but I've found it to be a place where people are more interested in dating than finding and developing long-term relationships."

Even though she still hopes to get married someday, Stacy cautions younger women to avoid rushing to the altar just for the sake of getting married, but rather to open their eyes to the deep value in building a relationship with the right one that could lead to marriage regardless of the timing. "It is worth finding the balance in career and relationship; the timing may never be ideal."

Stacy also says her strong faith in God has given her a helpful perspective on her singleness. "Everything happens for a reason, so I trust God and leave this in his hands," she explains. "I take great comfort from a verse in Isaiah 54: 'For your Maker is your husband—the Lord Almighty is his name' (v. 5). Who am I to argue with that? He knows far better than I on all of this, and I am so very thankful to know him."

5

when your world collapses

IT MAY NOT HAPPEN TO YOU. I hope it doesn't. But it might. In fact, there's about a fifty-fifty chance that it will.

In January 1997, the divorce that I filed for — the divorce I never wanted to happen — was signed, sealed, and approved by the State of Oklahoma. It is an event in my life that I'm not proud of. If you haven't already figured it out, I'm a results-oriented individual. I was taught — and I truly believed — I could do anything. Valedictorian of my Oregon State University graduating class of 4000. MBA from Harvard. As I write this, my parents have been married for fifty-four years. Divorce just didn't happen to people like me.

If filing those papers that would end our marriage was devastating, receiving them back as final, official proof that our marriage was over only put an exclamation mark on a horrible feeling: I had failed!

Suddenly I was a single mom with a five-year-old and a seven-year-old and a demanding job. I hated the fact that my kids would join the 37 percent of American children who would grow up in a home without their biological father. I was angry that I hadn't seen some of the danger signals that my friends later told me were evident to them. Mostly, I was hurt. The man I fell in love with and enjoyed being with. The man who made me laugh and who was such a good father. The man I had planned to spend the rest of my life with. This man to whom I gave myself had shown by his dishonest actions that he clearly no longer wanted to be with me.

Can't We Just Skip This?

I hesitated sharing this chapter of my life for a lot of reasons. For one, it hurts on so many levels. No one likes to admit that their spouse made choices that would make their marriage end. And being raised in the church, I had been taught that marriage is for life. Then there's the fact that the wonderful children who were a product of this marriage don't exactly need to have their parents' problems put out there for everyone to see. It's not like they didn't experience a world of hurt too.

I also considered glossing over this part of my story because it could be too easy to focus on blame and paint my former husband as some kind of monster. He wasn't and isn't. We just shouldn't have gotten married in the first place. Yes, it's hard to admit that, especially since in the business world I'm pretty good at reading people and making a plan. However, my plan was not his plan, and I completely misread him.

How could I be so successful in other areas up until age thirty-seven, yet fail at one of the most important things in life?

This is why I decided to share this painful story with you. Time not only heals wounds, but gives perspective. I so wish I could give you some sort of guarantee that if you apply this formula, you'll have a happy and long-lasting marriage. I can't. But maybe I can pass along a few guiding principles that will help you beat the fifty-fifty odds that all of us are given when it comes to marriage.

Guiding Principles When Dating

Don't be in a hurry. I didn't exactly rush into marriage, but once I thought I found Mr. Right, I pretty much decided this was the guy. As I look back, even though we were engaged for over a year, we didn't spend a lot of time together. I honestly believe if we would have waited to get married until after I finished at Harvard, things might have turned out differently.

Beware long-distance romance. I know things are different today with cell phones, texting, email, Skype, and other ways to stay in touch, but face-to-face communication is the only real way to get to know someone. While dating, during our engagement, and the first several months of our marriage, I was in New Jersey and Massachusetts, and he was in Oklahoma. I was too naïve to realize I was giving him opportunities that he probably didn't need. Yes, you can argue that trust ought to be enough, but practically speaking, being separated for long periods of time invites other things to happen when you are apart.

Pay attention. Another good argument against long-distance relationships is the few times you are together, you're just so happy and excited that you will miss important signs that later seem obvious. I really didn't know who my fiancé's real friends were, who he hung out with, and what he did for fun when I wasn't around. And I wasn't around a lot.

Do your due diligence. It's amazing how carefully we check out a business before we buy it compared to how we check out the person we hope to spend our lives with. After our divorce, several of my friends told me they weren't surprised and then went on to share some things I wished I had known before we got married. I know that in the joy and excitement of being engaged, we don't like to ask tough questions of our friends ... and they aren't likely to volunteer any information that might seem critical or judgmental. But at least go to your most trusted friends and see what they *really* think. Breaking off an engagement is a lot easier than going through a divorce.

Go with your gut. I honestly did not have any misgivings or second thoughts as my wedding day approached. But I know people who have, and my counsel is for you to listen to the deepest corners of your heart. If what you hear raises doubts, look for the emergency brake.

Be honest with yourself. Why are you getting married? I don't think I really asked myself that question, and here's where our greatest strengths can become a weakness. I was big on execution. Getting things done. In many ways—especially when I was just getting started in my career—life was a series of checklists, and marriage was on the list. If you're engaged or about to become engaged, here are three "why" questions I recommend you spend some time thinking about:

1. Why am I getting married?
2. Why am I marrying this man?
3. Why am I marrying this man now?

And if all your answers are, "because I love this man," I have one more question for you to wrestle with: why? If you can't answer that one with some specifics, you may just be in love with love.

What If?

You might think that going through a divorce has soured me on marriage. Not in the least. And I hope sharing about my divorce hasn't added to any skepticism or distrust of marriage. Going through my divorce taught me that my contentment must come from God, not from my spouse; he is just frosting on the cake. While I do not believe a woman needs a husband in order to be fulfilled as a human being, I'm a big fan of marriage and through God's grace and providence, I am today married to a wonderful man and enjoying it immensely. I love being able to share the joys as well as the struggles of life with my husband as we both share the pleasure of nurturing our two families into one exotic blend.

And yet I know that there is a possibility that you have either experienced a divorce or face one in the future, so here's what I wish someone would have told me as I was going through mine:

You are not a failure. Our—emphasis on *our*—marriage failed. But that didn't make me a failure. It's important that you not let divorce or even the circumstances surrounding it define you. Trust me; you will struggle with enough emotional distress that you don't need to beat your-self up. Remind yourself that you are the same person with the same God, the same extended family and children, the same gifts, the same educa-tion, and the same opportunity to succeed as you were before the divorce.

Avoid the blame game. I have seen too many women become bitter over their divorces and take every opportunity they can to paint their ex-husbands in the worst possible light. Other than making themselves look bad, this accomplishes nothing. If you make him look bad, you make yourself look bad because you loved him at one point. Because we had children, I did not want these innocent people to hate their daddy; therefore, I tried to make sure I never said bad things about him. I wasn't always perfect at this—one time they heard me call him a jerk. But even if children aren't involved, you are doing yourself a huge favor by not getting caught up in blame.

Find the good in every bad situation. The more you focus on the nega-tive, the longer it will take you to recover. Despite the way it ended, my marriage provided a lot of joy—as well as two wonderful children. My former husband and I seldom fought and we had a lot in common, enjoy-ing many special days and events that still provide good memories. If all I did was focus on the betrayal, I do not think I would be in the good place that I am today. In addition, I needed to be a much more compas-sionate, sympathetic, and sensitive person. These were some of my big weaknesses and are still areas I need to improve today. But going through the divorce, I grew in these areas of weakness.

Seek out support. I don't know what I would have done without the help of a few very close friends who were there to listen, to comfort me, to let me cry on their shoulders. One of them, Sue Bird, was my angel. Sometimes support will come from the unlikeliest places too. I'll never forget how I dreaded having to tell my boss, George, that I was filing for divorce. I knew I might not be all that focused at work and wanted to explain why. His compassionate response became a source of strength for me as I began to see that just maybe I might get through this.

Lean on your faith. Through this and other difficult times, I have learned that God is closest to us when we feel furthest from him. He uses disappointment and discouragement to help us grow, but only if we turn to him and open our hearts to him. My tendency as a problem solver was to just bear down and figure out a way to move forward, but real growth came when I invited God to walk through this difficult journey with me. He comforted me with the song "You Are My All in All," which ran through my head hourly. To this day, I can hardly sing the song without tearing up. It got me through a lot. I also found help through reading *The Road Less Traveled* by M. Scott Peck. It reminded me that those who leaned on their faith during tough times made it through much better than those that didn't.

Take care of yourself. I've always been a huge advocate for exercise—I run every morning. But it is especially important that you exercise, eat well, and get your rest whenever you go through emotional trauma. A lot of women retreat into unhealthy behavior during times of stress—overeating, drinking too much, and/or moping around. Good physical health is a strong ally for good emotional health.

Moving On

I really wish I hadn't had to write this chapter. As much as I feel I've grown—and as happily married as I am today—there's still a small part of me that hates to admit I failed. But maybe my story will help you realize that it's okay to make mistakes, even big ones. That it's often those things that brought us to our knees that gave us the greatest growth. The world in which we live and work doesn't always believe that. And when that thinking begins to creep into our lives, we miss out on the best that God has in store for us. It is that way of thinking that leads us to wear masks and pretend that everything is just fine, when we know it really isn't.

Perhaps the greatest lesson I learned from my divorce is that with God's help, I can face anything and come out on the other side a better person. You can too. But only if you allow yourself to be exactly who you are. To be authentic, not just when everything in your life is going as planned, but when things go horribly wrong. And they will.

I was tempted to hide this part of my story from you, but I chose to follow the advice I've always tried to live by: just tell the truth.

Sometimes it will help you. Sometimes it won't.

But it's always the right thing to do.

For Reflection and Discussion

1. When you hear the word *divorce*, what words or phrases come to mind?

2. Given that divorce is relatively common in our culture, why do people find it so difficult to talk about it? Why would the author consider leaving this part of her story out?

3. The author advises those who have experienced divorce to focus on the good. Do you think it is possible to find something good in every bad situation in life? Reflect on yours.

4. Who would you go to for support if you experienced a serious emotional trauma such as divorce, the loss of a loved one, the unexpected loss of a job? Why? What do you expect from a close friend or confidante in times of stress and sadness?

5. Despite her divorce, the author still believes in marriage. Do you? What are your honest thoughts about marriage? Do the statistics about divorce frighten or discourage you?

6. How has your faith or family tradition influenced your thoughts about marriage and divorce?

7. Do you think it is possible for a person to place too much emphasis on marriage? Why or why not?

single, married ... whatever

YOU WOULD THINK Trish would be one of the happiest people on earth. At thirty-one, she's the youngest in her firm's history to make partner, which nearly doubled her already generous salary. Her work has taken her overseas several times a year to places like Paris, Beijing, London, and Barcelona. Vivacious and attractive, she has no shortage of guys to choose from if she wants to enjoy dinner or dancing or a movie. So why, despite all the good things going on in her life, does Trish struggle with anxiety and a nagging sense of being unsettled?

"Most of my best friends are married and starting their families," she explains. "I've had two guys propose to me, but neither of them felt like the right guy, but then I'm starting to wonder if I would know the right guy if he jumped out in front of me. And then there's a part of me that has no desire whatsoever to get married. I wish I could just enjoy where I am right now, but it's getting complicated."

I've met a lot of young professionals like Trish. Single. Successful. But out of sorts. Perfectly eligible, they've chosen to remain single. At least for now. Yet most of their friends and associates have been to the

altar at least once, many with children entering school. There's that biological clock ticking loudly inside their heads, but they also enjoy the
freedom of being single. They're not opposed to getting married, but on
the other hand, they're not exactly thrilled with the odds. They've seen
their own parents split up, or someone else's, and that casts a chill over
the warm and fuzzy dream of the white-picket-fence marriage they one
day imagined.

Then there are women like Angela. She and her husband, Roger, have
been married for five years. Roger holds an executive-level position with
a manufacturing company, while Angela is a fashion buyer for a major
chain of retailers. Their solid marriage has begun to hit a few bumps in
the road during the last two years. Initially, only Angela had to travel for
her job; then a promotion for Roger put him on the road at least three
times a month, and always when Angela wasn't traveling.

"At first it didn't seem like a big deal, but now we see each other
less and less due to the travel, and whenever I bring it up, Roger gets
annoyed." Angela shrugged. "We don't really argue about it, and that's
almost worse because we just quit talking."

Then there was the issue of starting a family. For Angela, it wasn't
an issue. She didn't feel like it was time yet, so end of story. What's to
discuss? But Roger worried that if they waited too long, he would be an
old man by the time their kids entered high school (um, since when is
forty-something an old man?). Unlike the travel issue, this one ignited
some heated arguments, the intensity of which surprised Angela.

"When we got married, we vowed we'd never argue like other couples
do, yet here we were yelling at each other over starting a family."

If you read the preceding chapter, you know I'm not an expert on
marriage, but in talking with so many young professional women it
became clear to me that the whole intertwining issue of marriage and
singleness is a big deal and needs to be addressed. Three major questions
seem to pop up: what's wrong with being single, how do you make sure
he's the right guy, and how do you stay married?

What's Wrong with Being Single?

Absolutely nothing, as more and more women are discovering. According to data from the U.S. Census Bureau, for the first time in history, there are more single women than married women. That doesn't necessarily mean that women are choosing singleness over marriage, just that they are postponing the bridal shower. Linda Manning, former director of Vanderbilt University's Margaret Cuninggim Women's Center, reports that in 1950, 42 percent of fifteen- to twenty-four-year-old women were married, whereas today, less than 16 percent are.

"The period of adolescence is taking longer for most people," Manning said. "They are living at home longer, they are getting more education. They're delaying marriage for all of those reasons." The article also referred to another reason women are staying single longer: "She wants to make sure she does it right the first time."[1]

Being a single woman no longer carries with it the stigma that there must be something wrong with you if you aren't married by the time you're twenty-one. Still, the single life for a young professional woman who wants to honor God can be challenging. I hope this doesn't sound old-fashioned or judgmental, but the Bible's teaching about chastity doesn't exactly play well to the *Sex and the City* world where all single adults are "players." In *Real Sex*, a wonderful book that I would highly recommend to any single woman, Lauren Winner writes, "Chastity is one of the many Christian practices that are at odds with the dictates of our surrounding, secular culture. It challenges the movies we watch, the magazines we read, the songs we listen to. It runs counter to the way many of our non-Christian friends organize their lives. It strikes most secular folk as curious (at best), strange, backwards, repressed."[2]

In other words, just about everyone else *is* doing it. According to a study published in *Public Health Reports*, by age twenty, 75 percent of Americans have engaged in sex before they marry; by age forty-four, the percentage jumps to 95.[3] I'm not so naïve as to believe that every single woman who loves God is part of that minority who has chosen chastity. Every woman has to decide for herself how she is going to negotiate the issues of sexual intimacy in her relationships. And for those who set high standards and make mistakes along the way, God's forgiveness and limitless grace is wonderfully healing. I only raise this issue because I know so many single Christian women struggle with it. At the risk of sounding preachy, here are some very simple guidelines that will help you in this important area:

God's guidelines are always for our own good. He doesn't ask us to reserve sex for marriage because he's a dour, repressive killjoy. He wants the best for us—to protect us from the emotional pain and other consequences that often accompany the kind of freewheeling sex we see in our culture.

You control your own body. Just because some guy thinks you should sleep with him doesn't mean you have to. *Cosmopolitan* magazine reports a phenomenon they call "gray rape"—sex between acquaintances where the girl clearly indicated she didn't want to have sex but the guy continued, leaving the girl in a moral "gray area": Did I consent by going along with it? Was it my fault because I didn't refuse forcefully enough?[4] These aren't random acts with strangers, but people who know each other well and are in a relationship. You set your standards, no one else.

Grace is free and healing. Single Christian women who have found themselves in intimate relationships often struggle with guilt and shame because they know they are missing out on God's ideal for them. Through God's forgiveness and grace we can reclaim his ideal and experience his gift of purity; we can walk away from the mistakes of our past and actually become "a new creation" (2 Corinthians 5:17).

How Do You Make Sure He's the Right Guy?

I'm well aware that not every single woman is looking to get married, and that's fine. I don't believe you have to be married to be fulfilled as a woman; I've known many single women who are perfectly happy and content with their lives. However, I also have known younger single women who would like to be married but worry they will make the wrong choice: "I don't want to wake up someday and realize I married the wrong guy!" they say.

I wish there was a foolproof way for you to find Mr. Right, but men don't come with guarantees (neither do we, for that matter). Both in my own experiences and in observing others, I think a lot of us get caught up in the moment with all the romance and excitement of meeting someone who seems to be The One that we temporarily abandon our common sense. I'm all for romance, but if you want to increase your chances of finding a guy who will be with you "till death do us part," slow down a little and ask yourself the following questions:

Does he believe the same way I do? The Bible warns against being "yoked together with unbelievers" (2 Corinthians 6:14). If the guy you're interested in doesn't share your faith in Christ, it's a deal breaker. Don't make the mistake many women do and think you'll win him over. It seldom happens. If you are not aligned at this core level, it will become a constant source of tension.

Does he value the same things I value? In addition to your faith, are the things that are important to you important to him? Does he enjoy being with your family or does he always find an excuse to skip out of those functions? If you're passionate about the arts, does he support that? Opposites attract at first, but eventually they drift apart.

Am I overlooking any warning signs? Does he have a temper? Does he always seem to need a drink when you go out socially? Does he flirt with other women? Sometimes we see things like this and brush them off because we're so in love with the guy. If you see something that troubles you, can you talk with him about it? If not, what makes you think it won't be a problem after the honeymoon?

What do my family and friends think about him? It's tough to please Dad, but pay attention to what he has to say about the guy you bring home. And don't be afraid to ask a close sister or friend, "What do you *really* think of him?" If they care about you, they'll tell you the truth, and if you're smart, you'll listen. I can't tell you how many times I've heard a friend say, "I saw that coming" after news of someone's divorce.

How does he treat me? This may seem obvious, but I'm amazed at how many young women become serious with guys who treat them poorly. I don't think it's old-fashioned to expect a guy to treat a woman with respect. If he's rude to you, insults you in front of your friends, never opens a door for you, don't waste your time.

If you answer these questions honestly, you may find a few chinks in the armor of Sir Galahad, and that's okay. No one's perfect—some women remain single and frustrated about it because, quite frankly, they're looking for the perfect man. He doesn't exist. Pondering these questions can open the door to one other important "test" to help ensure that the guy you're interested in is all that you hope he is: honest conversation. Trust me; once you're married, you will have plenty of occasions where you need to talk about tough stuff. If the two of you can talk honestly and dispassionately about some of the concerns you might have, that's a good sign that he is secure and willing to work on the rough edges. To be fair, he ought to be able to bring up things about you as well without you throwing a hissy fit. It's easy being married when everything is rosy and nice. The real test comes when you have to have those difficult conversations.

You're not perfect, and you won't find a perfect man to be your husband. But you can find a guy who's perfectly compatible with you if you combine a little common sense with all that love and romance.

How Do You Stay Married?

Every now and then I'll be in a grocery store or walking down the sidewalk and I'll see an elderly couple holding hands. They could be in their eighties and barely able to walk, but they're holding hands like a couple of teenagers in love. How cool is that?

If you could ask ten different couples like that the secret to staying married for so long, you'd likely get ten different answers. Once when former *Today Show* weatherman Willard Scott showcased a couple who had been married for seventy years, he said they stayed married that long because they went out dancing every Friday night! If there really was a secret or fail-safe formula for staying married, divorce would be obsolete, because I've never met a married couple who didn't start out with a fervent desire to remain married forever.

From a lot of reading on the subject, great counseling, learning from people who've seen at least their silver wedding anniversary, and my own experience, I can share a few things that seem to be the common denominators to successful marriages.

Good marriages don't just happen. They require regular attention. Over and over again I hear this from people who are happily married: "Marriage is hard work." Chris and I regularly go over our finances together, which helps, but it's not enough. We also have to regularly ask ourselves, "How are we doing being married?" Taking stock of your marriage is a lot like early detection of a serious disease. It allows you to recognize little concerns before they grow into huge, insurmountable problems.

Communication. Communication. Communication. Nearly every marriage expert considers this the most important factor in a successful marriage. Good communication is more than just having a nice conversation over dinner. It's making sure you regularly schedule time together just to talk and listen. To get caught up and reacquainted. Communication also means you take every opportunity you can to express your love and affection to each other. Few things make a guy happier than to hear his wife say, "I'm so proud of you!"

Be careful about criticism. Few things take the shine off a relationship quicker than criticism. That doesn't mean you shouldn't address legitimate concerns, but if you're not careful, criticism can almost become a habit. Two approaches have been extremely helpful to me. First, don't make everything a hill to die on. Second, try to turn your criticism into a compliment. For example, instead of saying, "I'm sick and tired of the way you always leave your clothes on the floor," consider this: "You can't believe how much it helps me when you hang your clothes up." And by the way, avoid words like *always* and *never*.

Continue dating. Another "no-brainer," but you'd be surprised how many couples quit dating after they get married. And then they wonder why they drift apart. In case you've forgotten, dating means just the two of you doing something you both enjoy. Most couples quit dating once they start a family, and that's the *most* important time to keep dating. Once you give up that time together, it's hard to program it back into your schedules. I heard somewhere that there's been an increase in divorce among people who've been married for more than twenty years. Reason? They focused so much on their children that once the nest was empty they had nothing in common to keep them together. Don't let that happen to you.

Kiss and make up early and often. "Do not let the sun go down while you are still angry" (Ephesians 4:26). You're both going to make mistakes and disappoint each other. When you do, make it right as soon as possible. The longer you hold back an apology or forgiveness, the more damage it will do to your relationship.

Give each other space. I don't expect Chris to tag along when I head out for some fun (for me at least) bargain shopping at secondhand stores, and when he wants to retreat in the living room and get lost in a good book, I've learned to leave him alone. At first, I had a tendency to want him to use that time to work on some projects around the house, but I finally just told myself to chill out and let him have what he needs. Healthy relationships thrive from both togetherness and time apart. Marriage isn't a prison sentence where you're stuck in a cell with someone for the rest of your life.

Keep the playful spirit alive. A married couple was enjoying lunch at a restaurant. As they were eating, a gentleman who had been sitting near them approached and said, "You two can't possibly be married — you're having way too much fun." What a sad commentary about the popular perception of marriage. Lighten up. Don't ever grow up or act your age. In their book *The Love List*, marriage experts Les and Leslie Parrott write, "The more you laugh together, the more you love your spouse."[5]

Get help when you need it. Couples who want to stay married are never hesitant to seek guidance from professional counselors or mentors. Most churches either provide both or partner with local counseling clinics. Additionally, organizations such as Marriage Enrichment, Inc. (www.marriageenrichment.org) and Marriage Encounter (www.wwme .org) provide weekend events to help strengthen marriages — think of them as tune-ups for your marriage. Chris and I attended "A Weekend to Remember" conference put on by FamilyLife (www.familylife.com) about four years into our marriage when we needed a tune-up. It brought us together and helped us both focus on areas we could both work on. About three years later, we needed another tune-up, so when Chris asked me what I wanted for Christmas, I said, "I don't want anything except for us to have a more fulfilling marriage." When Chris moved forward and found a counselor that he saw and then we both saw together, those actions spoke volumes to me.

. . .

If you're single and enjoy where you are right now, don't cave in to pressure from family and friends to get married. That's almost a sure recipe for a failed marriage. If you're single primarily because you're afraid to make the mistakes your divorced parents or friends made, let your fears work for you by approaching dating with your head as much as with your heart. And if you're married, I know that deep within your soul you want to someday be that tottering old couple holding hands in the grocery store.

I offer no guarantees, but here's a clue: Whose hand are you holding in the grocery store now?

For Discussion and Reflection

1. In what ways do you think contemporary culture has shaped your view of singleness and marriage? Are those views different from the views of your parents? Explain.
2. Single men in their twenties and thirties are often said to have a fear of commitment. Is this a distinctly male issue or do you think women in the same age range have a similar fear?

3. If you are married—or single but plan to be married someday—
   what are the qualities you most admire in a husband? Why?

4. What could the church do to better serve young single women?
   What could *you* do to help the church do a better job serving
   young single women?

5. The rate of divorce for people of faith is almost identical to the
   rate of divorce among couples who are not Christians. Why do
   you think Christians have as much difficulty staying married as
   non-Christians? What can you do to have a better chance of not
   being that statistic?

6. Among the married people you have known, who do you most
   admire for the way they relate to each other as a couple? Why?

7. Describe the ways you have sought help when you were having
   difficulty with your relationship with a boyfriend or husband.
   What other things would you be willing to try to tune up your
   relationship?

Is He the Right One for Me?

You're dating a guy, he seems like he might be the one, but you're not sure. Now what? According to Lisa Gardner, CEO and entrepreneur, you begin with his faith.

"Make sure he has the same maturity of faith and commitment to spiritual growth that you do," Gardner advises. "That is the foundation that will take your marriage to where it ought to be."

It is that foundation that gave her Lawrence, her husband of fourteen years, and two children. Along the way she has held key positions with companies such as Frito-Lay, Pepsi, and JCPenney.

In addition to sharing a common faith in Christ, Gardner believes couples should talk openly and honestly about the things that often become problems in marriage: finances, how to prioritize their lives, how to raise their children.

"Show each other your credit reports, and if it reveals some problems, talk about them. If you can't talk about these things now, it won't get any easier after you're married."

Gardner also cautions young professional women to be flexible about their future plans.

"When I got married, my singular goal was to become a top executive in a big corporation — which I was able to do, but soon God gave me a burden to start our family. God called me out of the corporate world to grow me as a wife, mother, and woman of God. After taking some time off and then earning an MBA, I sensed God calling me back into the business world, only this time to start my own consulting firm with the balance of priorities in order."

The name of Gardner's firm, OMS (for Order My Steps from Psalm 119:133) Strategic Advisors, reflects her belief that if you put your trust in God, he will guide you in the path that is best for you. She and Lawrence have mentored young couples for several years and have this advice for those who not only want to get married, but stay married:

"Surround yourself from the beginning with married couples who are more mature in Christ than you, and when you run into problems—and you will—go to them for help. That's what we did, and we still seek out these older couples whenever we run into difficulties in our marriage."

the truth will
open some doors . . .
and close others

IN A TIGHT JOB MARKET with the economy in the tank, Sarah was just glad to get the interview. When she entered law school four years earlier, graduates with brand-new degrees and no experience were being swooped up by major law firms who lured them with big salaries and the promise of a rapid rise toward making partner. How quickly things change. When Sarah entered the job market, few firms were hiring, and those that were couldn't be blamed for choosing lawyers with a few years experience who recently had been let go by other firms who were cutting back. Most of her classmates began taking jobs outside the legal profession because they needed to begin paying back student loans — even a small income was better than no income. So Sarah was almost too embarrassed to tell Nicole, her best friend and study partner throughout law school, about the interview.

As she stepped into the elevator, she took a deep breath and let it out slowly to calm her nerves as she mentally prepared for the interview. She knew she was one of three candidates for the job, and given the current job market, she knew she may not get another chance for quite a while. When the elevator door opened and she saw the big glass doors of the law firm, she remembered the advice given to her by her favorite professor: "Just be yourself."

The interview seemed to go well as she gained confidence with each question. Then came the one that stumped her: "Sarah, we're a pretty fast-paced firm and we expect a lot from all our attorneys. Typically, for the first two to three years, you'll be looking at sixty- to seventy-hour weeks. Are you comfortable with that?"

Unlike most of her classmates, Sarah was married and had a three-year-old daughter and had always planned on finding a job that left her evenings and weekends free. She wasn't sure how she should answer that question. She needed the job. If she hesitated or attempted to negotiate, she knew there were two other candidates who probably didn't mind the long hours. If she told a little white lie, and said she was comfortable with the extra work, what would happen the first time her husband, a surgeon, couldn't pick their daughter up at the preschool?

The Truth about Families and Work

Beginning in the 1960s, the number of women entering the workplace has grown at a phenomenal rate—from about 40 percent of women aged 25–54 to about 77 percent in the mid–1990s. And then it stalled and has actually decreased somewhat, to about 75 percent in 2006. Why? According to Suzanne M. Bianchi, a sociologist from the University of Maryland who has studied the amounts of time women spend working inside and outside of the home, many women with children are leaving the workplace because it's just too much work.[1]

I have to be honest with you. Families take time. Parenting is not for the faint of heart, whether you work outside of the home or not. At every stage your children experience—from infancy until they learn to fly on their own—they require time and energy, and if you're like most moms, you are totally willing to give them all that they need. I know what it's like to be up all night with a sick baby or a troubled teen and still have to go to work the next day and wade through the deep waters of difficult negotiations, arduous meetings, and sticky personnel issues. I also know that there are many times when your family needs you during your normal work hours — parent-teacher conferences, doctor and dentist appointments, after-school sports and music events. If you have already begun a family, you know what I mean. If you haven't but plan to, you will.

Decisions, Decisions

Obviously, I'm assuming that you either have children or plan to start a family someday, but many couples are deciding not to have children. Ever. While the number of couples who chose not to have children is difficult to determine, it does seem to be increasing, according to a report by David Popenoe and Barbara Dafoe Whitehead, two nationally prominent family experts. "One out of five women in her early forties is childless compared to one in ten in 1980," they write. They also point out that young women are now more likely to put off starting a family so that they can complete their schooling and get established in their careers.[2] And according to the National Center for Health Statistics, the number of single-child families has doubled since the 1960s.[3]

All this to say, your options are far greater than they were for most women in my generation. It was pretty much assumed that within a year or two of getting married, a couple would start their family. But with increasing opportunities for women in the workplace, safer and more reliable methods of contraception, and the uncertainties of the economy, you now have a lot more choices. Do I set my career aside for a few years and start our family? Do we wait until we both have advanced degrees and good jobs before we have kids? Instead of two or three kids like our parents had, why not just have one? For that matter, why have any at all? And what happens when *he* wants to start a family but *I* don't?

I can't answer those questions for you. And neither can you. At least not alone. The whole area of family planning is the ultimate joint venture, requiring honest communication between you and your husband—if possible, before you get married.

"What Do You Think about Family?"

The decision to start a family also raises another important question: How do I communicate my priorities to my prospective employer without ruining my chance to get the job? Let me recap my story a bit to explain in more depth how I dealt with that question.

From the time I headed off to college, I knew that I wanted a career, but I also knew that I would one day want to have a family of my own. Growing up as I did in a close and loving family convinced me that being a wife and a mom was important to me. Maybe I developed an unrealistic attitude about balancing work and family because although my mom worked, she was always there for me because her work was our family farm. But it gave me a model that shaped who I am as a woman, convincing me that I could pursue a career and still enjoy a family.

To be honest, though, I never really thought a lot about balancing my family and my work until I arrived in Tulsa, Oklahoma, with my new master's degree and a husband with his own business. I knew I needed to find work—not so much for the money but because I really felt I had something to offer and wanted to use my gifts and talents to help others. So when I interviewed with a consulting firm, it was my first step toward what I hoped would be a rewarding blend of career and family, and I was determined to do it right.

Just like Sarah, my job interview went extremely well. I could tell that I was making a good impression, and as I learned more about the job, I sensed it was a pretty good fit. As the interview appeared to be winding down, the VP who was interviewing me leaned forward and said, "Well, Diane, we've asked *you* a lot of questions. Is there anything you want to ask about *us*?"

If you're ever asked that question, by the way, make sure you're prepared for it and have a few of your own questions ready. This is often yet another way for the company to test you—to learn more about you and the type of employee you might be. If you don't have any questions, it could appear that you are indifferent or uninterested in their company and that will work against you. Besides, if you're about to sign on with this outfit, you'd better know exactly what you're getting into.

I had a question, one that I always work into my job interviews in one form or another.

"What do you think about family?"

As much as I really wanted this job, I knew that Stan and I would soon be starting a family, and I felt it was important to know their views on family as it related to work. This was also my way of inviting a dialogue with them about the importance of family to me and what that meant in terms of how I would do my job. I explained to them that if the job required a lot of overnight travel or if I would regularly be expected to work evenings and weekends, I wouldn't be a good fit for their company.

"That's a great question, Diane," he said, much to my relief. "I'm so glad you asked it. In this particular position, you won't have to do any overnight travel. And while the job may occasionally require you to work more than forty hours a week, we can be flexible."

It was all I needed to hear. When they called later and offered me the job, I took it!

Like most women starting out, it took me a few years to find my stride. I discovered that consulting wasn't really for me even though my boss was pleased with my performance. One of my clients—a big health-care company—offered me a position and once again, I shared with them my priorities during the interview process. They too understood and supported my commitment to my family, so I accepted their offer and found myself in a challenging environment that seemed to be a good match for my skills.

I've always felt that if I'm going to establish boundaries between my work and my faith and my family, I need to make sure that when I am at work, I give 110 percent. Part of that comes from the farm, where I never wanted anyone to think the boss's daughter got off easier than anyone else. But I'm also just wired that way. If you have enough confidence in me to offer me a job and honor my priorities, I'm going to make you really glad you hired me. Plus, I love discovering ways to make a business grow.

I might have stayed in health care all these years except for the fact that my employer didn't have a pay-for-performance culture and that was important to me. I contacted two of my best friends from college and they convinced me to join them in a huge commercial real estate company, Trammell Crow/CB Richard Ellis, and that's where I stayed for over twenty years. Again, Trammell Crow was a family-friendly company. I shared my boundaries with them before I signed on: travel could only average one night a week away from home, and I would leave the office to be home to eat dinner with my family at six. That didn't mean I quit work totally when I left the office. When the kids were busy with school work, activities, or friends, I worked at home. It worked until I left the company in May of 2008. I had risen to be the Chief Operating Officer of Global Service for Trammell Crow Company and President of Client Accounts and Corporate Services, for CB Richard Ellis. A wonderful plus was that my colleagues had really become my friends—almost like family.

Hiding Your Convictions

Over the years I've known women who cared deeply about their families but took jobs they knew would put pressure on those relationships. In some cases, they were afraid to negotiate some boundaries when they were interviewing for their jobs because they thought it would keep them from getting the job; in other cases, they felt the company really didn't have any business knowing about their private lives. In both cases, these women felt they would somehow find ways to balance their demanding jobs with their family responsibilities but ended up having serious problems at work *and* at home. Here's how it usually happens:

You go to your interview all excited about a new job. The more you learn about your roles and responsibilities, you realize that they're going to expect a lot from you. But in a way, you like that because it means they have a lot of confidence in you and trust you with a big project. You also *love* everything about the company. They're cutting edge, leaders in their fields — even if you stayed only a couple of years, it would look great on your resume. As you get to meet some of your future colleagues, you begin to pick up on some other things that give you pause: "This is a great place to make a lot of money, but you'll *earn* it." "The hours are a pain, but it's such a great company and you'll be working on some really exciting projects." "You're gonna love it here, but you might want to keep a sleeping bag in your closet."

All the warning signals are there, waving in your face like a big red flag, but you keep your worries to yourself because it *does* sound like an exciting job that could lead to bigger and better things, and besides, you'll figure out what to do if it really does get as frenetic as they say it does. And maybe they're exaggerating.

So you take the job.

And then it starts happening. The first time you're late picking up your son from preschool, you feel horrible. The preschool workers make it clear they're annoyed with you, and seeing your son all alone and waiting for his mamma tears your heart out. So the next time you know your day is going to stretch way past six o'clock, you frantically call your husband at work and ask him to rush over to the preschool. He does, and even agrees to change his office hours so that your son always gets picked up on time, but that just makes you feel worse because you know you're allowing your job to take priority over your family.

Trust me; it's always better to be absolutely truthful about your priorities when interviewing for a new job. Even though things have gotten better in the workplace, it's still afflicted with this sense that the real players in any company put work ahead of everything else in their lives and almost wear their seventy-hour weeks as a badge of courage. This isn't just a male thing. As women began to nudge up against the glass ceiling in the 1970s and take their places beside men in leadership positions, they weren't about to play the "child card" and seek special favors when it came to things like after-hours work and travel. The result is a work environment—especially in professional, salaried positions—that is anything but nine to five.

But I Really Need the Job

Do you run the risk of not getting the job if you acknowledge that family comes first for you? Yes, and in a difficult job market or if you are the sole breadwinner for your family, holding firmly to those priorities may not be in your best interest. As a parent, one of your primary responsibilities is to care for the physical needs of your children—to make sure they have food, clothing, shelter, and a decent education. There will be times in your career when you may need to just bite the bullet and take a job that is not "family friendly" in order to keep your family fed and the bills paid. This is especially true for single moms or in families where the husband has lost his job.

If you really need a job and the only one being offered will require you to be away from your family a lot, be up front with your children and let them know that until you can find a better job that meets your priorities, they will have to make some sacrifices. Even with my employers' support for my values, there were those many occasions when I had to travel more than I wanted to in a given period of time. By taking the time to explain my temporary absence, my family was able to make adjustments and actually came closer together because of it. There's just something about everyone pitching in to help mom in her new job that develops a sense of camaraderie and "shared mission" in a family.

Just keep looking though, because eventually the clash between your values and your work will take its toll. As we will discover in the next chapter, more and more companies are finding ways to accommodate the values of their employees, but if you don't make those known up front, you can't expect them to be honored.

For Reflection and Discussion

1. To what extent should companies support or accommodate the personal values of their employees? Explain.

2. Assuming that you desire to have a career that does not sacrifice your family, what are some specific expectations you would have of your employer?

3. Your daughter is singing a solo in her high school choir concert which falls on the same night your boss wants you to join him and a key potential customer for dinner. What do you do?

4. If you were the CEO of a company, what kind of policy would you put in place for employees who wanted to leave work early to watch their kids' sports activities?

5. In most two-income families, the woman—by an overwhelming majority—assumes primary responsibility for nurturing children and household chores such as cooking and laundry. Why do you think this is true?

6. If you have children, how much time each day do you sit and talk with them? How would it affect your daily schedule if you made that a high priority?

7. What are your boundaries? How much are you willing to travel? Work late in the evening?

8. What are some solutions that you might be able to negotiate in order to spend more time with your family?

Balance Requires Discipline

Don't blame Rachel Shephard if she's feeling a little schizo-phrenic. She grew up being told she could do anything, be anything. Then once she finished college, she felt this not-so-subtle pressure to get married, have lots of babies, and stay home to care for them.

"Maybe someday, but right now I feel called to use my education and gifts to serve God in the marketplace," Rachel, an independent consultant for a major health and wellness company, explains.

Rachel recognized her own competitive nature and desire to succeed, so when she married Luke, they put some boundaries in place so that their work wouldn't squeeze the life out of their marriage.

"We both shared our goals and dreams for our respective careers to make sure we were both on board and supportive. Once a month we get out our calendars and schedule our lives around each other's busy times. In eight years of marriage I don't think we have ever missed a weekly date night where we shut off our cell phones and go out—just the two of us."

For single women who hope to find Mr. Right someday, Rachel has some very specific advice.

"If you're going to have a career, find a man who is secure in Christ—whose self-worth comes from God. Because Luke is confident in his relationship with Jesus, he doesn't get jealous about my ambitions but supports and encourages them. He wants me to succeed as much as I want him to succeed."

She also cautions single women to take their time and be choosy.

"It's better to be unhappily single than unhappily married," she warns.

Rachel and Luke established their priorities early on: their faith comes first, their marriage is second, and their careers are third. Balancing them becomes a matter of discipline, especially when it comes to career.

"The world tells us to strive for more and more money, so it's easy to get into that trap that leaves little time or energy for the two most important things in my life. I love my job and could work at it twenty-four/seven, but I choose to say no even if it means I might not earn as much as someone else."

What's the Plan?

Melissa and Chance Throop began planning their family before they were married. Even before they were engaged.

"I knew I would eventually want to have children, so it was important for me to find a spouse who shared that desire," Melissa, who is a commercial real-estate consultant, explains.

"I started out in accounting and then moved into telecommunications before accepting a position with the commercial real-estate firm Trammell Crow (now CBRE). I had been with Trammell Crow when I started an MBA program."

As she approached the end of her MBA program, Melissa was all set to get going on the family plan, but Chance was hesitant. He was finishing up school and wanted more stability before starting a family. Would Melissa be okay with that?

"At first, I was a little disappointed but it turned out to be one of the best decisions we've ever made. The worst thing a wife can do is pressure her husband to have a child. He needs to be fully engaged and just as eager as you are."

Melissa believes that couples need to start the family-planning conversation early and return to it often because everything from career moves to family finances can change without much notice.

"And it's not just when to start your family, but how you're going to raise your children," she advises. "Even before we were married we talked about how we would discipline our kids, what we would do about childcare, their religious education — it's so important that you're both on the same page about these things."

By the time Hayden entered their lives, they knew how they would share the responsibility of caring for her. Melissa negotiated being able to work from home on Fridays. Chance's student schedule gave him more flexibility to cover for Melissa when she travels. And they secured excellent day care for the times when neither can be at home during the day. Fortunately, they also have extended family nearby to give them a hand. "I have to be honest, though. It's hard work balancing a career with being a mom, and sometimes I struggle with guilt — especially when I see stay-at-home moms. But one real advantage is that because I don't get to be with her all day, every minute I'm with Hayden is special."

For Melissa and Chance, communication and flexibility is the key to their successful entry into parenthood. The original plan called for three, even four, children. Number two is on its way, but that's going to be it for the Throop family.

"What were we thinking?" she laughs.

finding compatible work environments

A MERE THREE MONTHS after accepting a generous offer from Trammell Crow to work for them, I discovered I was pregnant.

Great timing, right?

Of course my husband and I were thrilled with the news, but I wasn't sure my new company would be. Even though before I took the job I made it clear that my husband and I might be starting a family soon, I was a little nervous about telling my boss. If *I* hadn't planned on this happening quite this soon, I could only imagine what George would think. I knew that legally there was nothing they could do, but I'm not one to make "legality" my only standard when it comes to career issues. I never want to disappoint my colleagues, and I felt they might not appreciate my testing their family-friendly commitment so early.

Our offices in Tulsa were wide open, and the only way to have a private conversation is to find a conference room, so I walked over to George's desk and asked him to meet me in one.

"What's so confidential that we need to meet here?" George asked with a chuckle.

I took a deep breath and answered, "George, I'm pregnant."

All my anxiety faded immediately as he reached out to give me a big hug and offered his congratulations before adding, with yet another chuckle, "Wow! You did that a lot faster than I expected."

That was the beginning of a long tenure during which Trammell Crow proved over and over again to be a company that supports their employees' commitment to their families. Is my story unusual, or are there other companies like that? And if there are, how do you find them?

The Good News for Women

When I began my career a little over twenty years ago, women were just beginning to hit their stride in the marketplace. Consider some of these remarkable changes that have occurred in my lifetime. For example, in 1971 there were no women on the Supreme Court. By 2010 there were three. There were no female governors in 1971; six were serving in 2010. Only 3 percent of all lawyers were women in 1971; today, the percentage of women lawyers has grown to 37. For the first time in history, five women have won Nobel prizes in the same year. With the percentage of women in college (57 percent) surpassing the percentage of men (43 percent), more and more women are choosing to put their hard-earned (and expensive) education to work by choosing rewarding careers. For example, close to half of all law and medical degrees go to women (up from approximately 10 percent in 1970). Forty years ago, one-third of all workers were women; today there are more women than men in the workplace.

With so many of us out there adding value to the wide spectrum of businesses and other enterprises, employers have begun listening to us. Companies know that to attract the best workers from fully one-half of the talent pool, they need to find ways to accommodate women who have families. And they know that the trends point to even more women entering the workplace. More than 63 percent of new hires are women, and it has been estimated that by 2020, 75 percent of children will have mothers working outside of the home.[1] Consequently, an increasing number of businesses and other enterprises are adopting policies and practices that enable a woman to grow in her career without sacrificing her family's needs.

Family-Friendly Work Environments

One way that companies try to attract and retain employees is to create a family-friendly environment that especially appeals to working moms. Here are the most common features that would identify a company as family friendly:

Flextime. Twenty-nine percent of employees in the United States are now offered this option. Basically, you sign on for the usual forty hours a week but are given the flexibility to set your own hours (within reason). For example, the normal start time at your company might be 8:00 a.m. but as a mom with school-aged kids you want to be at home until they leave for school, so *your* start time might be 9:00 a.m. Obviously, you would be expected to make up that extra hour.

Reduced hours. Often a temporary arrangement allowing an employee to reduce her hours in order to have more time to care for her family. Combined with family leave (see below), it offers a helpful transition back to work for young mothers.

Telecommuting. This is a work arrangement allowing the employee to work part- or full-time at home, "commuting" via technology (email, phone, fax, teleconferencing, etc.).

Paid family leave. Under the Family and Medical Leave Act (FMLA), an employee may take up to twelve unpaid weeks off for the birth or adoption of a child, to care for a family member, or to recover from a serious physical illness. But many companies offer to pay the employee for part or all of this leave.

Job sharing. Two people share a full-time job, each working part-time.

On-site childcare. An increasing number of companies are establishing day-care facilities in their buildings, making it easier for working moms.

Compressed workweek. Some women opt for four ten-hour days, giving them a long weekend to spend time with their families.

Vouchers or subsidies for childcare. This financial assistance is specifically to pay for childcare.

Generous vacation time. Rather than the normal one- or two-week paid vacations that are offered to most entry-level employees, some companies have begun offering three- and four-week vacations to new employees.

Special parking for pregnant women. This may seem silly, but some companies reserve parking space closer to the building's entrance for pregnant women. By the seventh or eighth month, it doesn't seem silly at all!

The Heart behind the Policy

Almost as important as the policies a company might introduce to make it more family friendly is their attitude. When I was doing my graduate work, the business school frequently invited business leaders to speak or guest lecture. It was a great way to get an insider's view of a wide variety of businesses, so I attended those events whenever I could. I missed one, however, featuring a guy I had never heard of. According to my friends who heard this gentleman speak, he built a huge real-estate company from almost nothing. His formula for success: "I built my company on love."

I never forgot that statement, or the name of the guy who made it: Trammell Crow, the founder of the company that bears his name ... and the company that eventually became my home.

Companies are like people—they have their own distinct personalities. Usually the personality of the company comes from the people who work there, especially the senior leadership. I recently read of a large and successful car dealership in Kansas co-owned by two men. Because their own families were so important to them, they encouraged all of their employees to spend more time with their families, even prohibiting their salesmen from working more than thirty-six hours a week. That's unheard of in auto sales, but the owners believed their workers would be more productive at work if they lived happier lives at home. When they took over the dealership, it was selling thirty cars a month. In their first month of ownership, it sold one hundred cars. They attribute their success to their philosophy of putting families and the customer first.[2]

As you look for companies that will support your efforts to balance work and home, don't just look at their policies. Pay attention to the overall environment. It's often the little things that say a lot. Do you see pictures of family or children's artwork displayed in offices? What sort of reaction do you get when you mention you are married or that you have children? Are there any women on the leadership team? Are there many women your own age? Do employees seem friendly, relaxed? A company may have all the right policies for you as a working mom and still be unsupportive because of its personality. If the environment is tense — if it doesn't look like anyone's having fun — chances are you may face resentment from coworkers who do not qualify for family-friendly perks.

Recently I was interviewing for a job, and the CEO had just the right answers for all of my questions about the kind of environment I would find if I accepted the job. I have to admit that sometimes in those situations it feels almost too good to be true. After being together all day meeting some of the employees, I was driven back to the airport by a woman who had been with the company for quite some time. So I asked her what it was *really* like working for this company, and she basically echoed everything the CEO said. It pays to look beyond official policies and statements and try to discern the company's personality. Oh, by the way, that woman's name was Marla Maloney, and we've since become great friends (see sidebar on page 105).

Ages and Stages

As you grow and gain experience in your career, your family needs will change as well. If you have recently given birth, you know the challenges of combining your work and caring for an infant. For example, you may have excellent childcare and don't need to shorten your workday, but if you're breast-feeding, you will need some way to facilitate that (many companies provide private, comfortable rooms for nursing mothers). As your children enter school, you may find it necessary to negotiate for a flexible schedule so that you can attend the many important events that occur during the school day. The teen years generally provide you the opportunity to return to a somewhat normal schedule. But not always.

When my son hit his teenage years, he went through a period of rebellion — nothing more than what a lot of teens experience, but enough to get my attention. I knew that if I left him unsupervised from the time he got home from school until I got home from work, he might slip up. So I went to my boss and laid it all out for him, then asked him if I could work from home from 2:30 in the afternoon until the end of the day. Even though there was no formal policy covering this, he completely understood and gave me the green light to work at home as long as I needed to. Thankfully, this was a relatively short time frame, February to June. I can happily say that my son learned a lot through this troubling time. Now at twenty-two, he relies on his faith and understands that God is always there to guide him. But this experience illustrates that one size doesn't fit all when it comes to family-friendly solutions.

Family friendly doesn't always refer to our kids. For example, what kind of support can you expect from your company if your husband experiences a serious, long-term illness? What would happen if a parent has a stroke and you need to be there for them? Each stage of life brings potential challenges to our families that intersect with our careers. A company that is truly family friendly may not have a policy to cover every emergency or family need that arises, but they are quick to demonstrate they care and will do their best to find the right solution. I've learned that if you are always honest and let your supervisor know what's going on in your life, companies will be inclined to create win-win solutions.

What's *Your* Responsibility?

At the end of the day, businesses exist to earn a profit by serving their customers. They aren't here to help you nurture your family. That's *your* job. While there may be levels of altruism in companies, the primary reason for being family friendly is self-serving—they do it because it's good for their business. And the way it helps their business is by retaining good workers. In other words, if you want to increase your chances of having your company support you in your efforts to balance work and family, be the best at what you do.

In order to be able to negotiate for anything in the marketplace— whether you are a man or a woman—you need leverage, and that usually comes from a track record. This is why I counsel younger women who are just starting out—even if they don't think they will get married or start a family—to begin building an impressive work resume. The more successes you can point to in your work history, the more likely an employer will create a work environment tailored to your needs. The reverse is just as true: no one's going to bend over backward to help a slacker.

A few years ago a young woman who reported to me wanted to adjust her work schedule because of some issues she was dealing with in her personal life. She explained what was going on and it was clear that she needed to be given some time and flexibility to work on something that was important to her. She had not been with the company very long, and we really didn't have a policy in place that would allow her to adjust her schedule. However, everything about this young woman said winner. She was one of those employees who would finish a project ahead of schedule and then ask for more—the kind of worker that truly added value to the company. So it was easy for me to work with her to come up with the right schedule for this particular time in her life. I knew that in the long run, the company would win because we would have held on to a valuable employee. Was I doing it to be nice? I like to think I'm a nice person, but if she had been one of those employees who was always late and did substandard work, I probably wouldn't have been so "nice."

I made the decision because I wanted to keep a good worker. Of course I cared about her personal life, but my responsibility was to my company, not to her marriage and family.

Even though the companies I have worked for have supported my values of faith and family, I never felt like that support was a right that I was entitled to. Rather, they were generous *privileges* that I needed to *earn* by being a valuable employee—one that they literally couldn't live without. When you ask for any family-friendly accommodation, your supervisor is going to do a quick mental calculation that goes something like this: "If I say no, she might quit. Can I live with that? Will our division suffer without her?" If you have established yourself as a hard worker who delivers results, I can guarantee that your supervisor will do everything in her power to help you artfully balance your job with your family responsibilities.

For Reflection and Discussion

1. Given your current status (single, married, small children, etc.), describe the ideal work environment. How might that change in five years? Ten years?
2. What specific family-friendly policies are available to you at your current place of employment?
3. Describe your company's "personality." What is its attitude toward women with young children at home?
4. The author believes that family-friendly policies are privileges to earn rather than rights the company owes to its employees. Do you agree or disagree? Explain.
5. Finish this sentence: "My supervisor would not want to lose me because ..."
6. Would you feel comfortable talking with your employer about issues of family stress? Why or why not?

A Supportive Company

After five years of climbing the corporate ladder at Ford Motor Company, Marla Maloney knew she had to make a change. Despite a bright future ahead of her at Ford, it just didn't feel like the kind of environment that matched up to her values. Among other things, she knew that to continue her climb, she would have to move a lot, and she had already moved five times in five years. Married and about to start a family, she knew she couldn't do that.

"I'm grateful for my years at Ford," she explained. "But I needed to find a place that not only provided me an opportunity to grow, but supported the things that were important to me as a person."

She interviewed with a commercial real-estate company that would eventually become known as Cassidy Turley. She looked closely at them while they reciprocated—over five interviews all over several days.

"I was honest about wanting to be able to move up in the company without having to move all over the world, because my family was important to me. I also spent time with several of the executives outside the office and observed what was important to *them*, which is a great way to learn about the values of a company. It became clear that they valued many of the same things I did, especially the concept of giving back to their communities. I not only met highly professional leaders, but Little League coaches, board members of women's shelters, men and women active in their parishes. In fact, they made it clear that if I aspired to become a leader in the company, I would be expected to also give back to the community in whatever area I might be passionate about."

It was a good fit and she took the job, unaware of just how much she would learn about how supportive this company would actually be. When her second child, Lindsey, was born with severe complications and whisked away to another hospital, her world suddenly stopped.

"I was devastated, but like a good trooper, I didn't share what I was going through with anyone at work. But then after a couple of weeks a young woman who I had hired came to visit me in the NICU and I just let it all out, and that began a journey so remarkable it's hard for me to even talk about it."

Colleagues began showing up at her home bringing meals, filling the refrigerator, mowing the lawn, and doing whatever was needed so that Marla and her husband, Mark, could spend time by their daughter's bedside. Then as her maternity leave was coming to an end, her boss showed up and told her not to worry about work—that they were extending her paid maternity leave indefinitely.

"He basically told me they didn't want to see me at work, and that I wasn't to return until my daughter had been home for at least one month."

That took five months, but the paychecks kept coming, along with continuing expressions of support from her colleagues. Today, she balances the challenges of parenting a special-needs child with a demanding job, but she knows she might never had made it this far without the support of her company.

"I absolutely believe it's possible to find a work environment that is supportive of your values. When you're being interviewed, be honest about who you are, not just about what you do. You can't expect a company to support what's important to you if they don't know what that is."

Stay True to Your Core Values

Sometimes the business world can be a tough place to work. Just ask Toni Portman. A successful entrepreneur and CEO, Portman has enjoyed a stellar career as an executive in a variety of businesses. In one stint as a CEO, she took her company from $70 million in annual revenue to $600 million. Currently she's the chairperson of a high-tech company and also works with a private equity firm. But at least twice she walked away from her corner office because of her personal values.

"A new CEO arrived at the firm where I was a member of the leadership team, and I just couldn't be a part of the new environment he created," Portman explains. "His idea of entertaining clients was to hit the bars and strip clubs. And his way of motivating employees was to scream at them. While I was never the target of his tirades, I saw it happen a lot."

In another instance, Portman took a job with a company and by her own admission didn't do her homework about the company's work environment.

"Once I got settled into my position, I discovered a free-wheeling, almost chaotic environment where there was little accountability and even some questionable business practices from an ethical point of view."

In both cases, Portman left, and recommends others do the same if they find themselves in an environment that does not align with their values.

"You spend more time at work than anyplace else, and if your work environment clashes with who you are as a person, it drains you emotionally and spiritually. A career is more than a paycheck. It ought to be a place where you thrive and grow."

Portman distinguishes between values and the type of work you're expected to do.

"The worst job I ever had was actually the best job. As part of my career development I was put in charge of a department that was all about process and systems. As an outgoing, extroverted people person, I thought that job would kill me, but it added a dimension to my skill sets that ended up making me a better leader."

Her advice to a young woman just starting out in her career?

"Stay true to your core and never let your work or a boss force you to compromise."

trade on
your strengths

A FRIEND OF MINE shared this theory with me: most people with a fairly decent college education can do a lot of things reasonably well, but probably only one or two things *really* well. I completely agree. While going to college teaches you some specific information, what it really teaches you to do is to learn on your own. No one's around forcing you to do your homework or go to class. All those papers you had to write? What they *really* taught you was how to find the information you need (research), make some sense of it (analysis), and most important, meet a deadline (execution). That pretty much describes a lot of what we all do, regardless of our chosen profession. A lot of recruiters will say they don't care that much what a candidate majored in—just that she put in four years of hard work and has the good grades to show for it, with leadership activities being a very important ingredient.

Somewhere between your freshman year in college and a few years into your career, you will begin to discover those few things that you do extremely well, and these are the things you need to build on. If you're pretty good at meeting new people and interacting with them, but cringe at the thought of poring over spreadsheets to try and make sense out of them, don't waste too much time trying to boost your spreadsheet skills. Turn your people skills into your strongest asset by strengthening them and finding ways to use them in your current position.

That doesn't mean you ignore your weaknesses completely. I once had the opportunity to mentor a senior woman who worked for a commercial real-estate firm in a position that required very strong relationship-building skills with clients. She had wonderful process and project-management skills, but her people skills were deficient. At the time, her company was growing quickly in the area she led, but her company's leadership wasn't sure she was the right person for the job because of her poor people skills. By improving her people skills, she added to her strengths, and today, she is a leader in international account transitions and very successful.

Discovering Your Strengths

Whenever I have the opportunity to counsel younger people on career choices, I always tell them to start with what they enjoy doing. To me, the ideal career is to be able to do something you love to do and actually get paid for it. Most of us are going to spend twenty-five or more years working, so why not find something that is relatively easy for you (skills) and that you enjoy (interests)? Too often we choose to go into a particular area because of a college major or because of expectations from parents or peers, only to discover a few years into the job that it just doesn't fit who we are. I almost made that mistake because my major in college was fashion merchandising, but working in the industry one summer convinced me it didn't play to my strengths. The first step in building on your strengths is to ask yourself: What am I good at?

Human nature being what it is, though, we're not always honest with ourselves about our strengths and weaknesses. We like to think we're strong in a particular area when in fact that may not be an area of strength at all. Or we have false or inaccurate expectations of the skills needed for a particular career. That's why it's so important to engage in some honest and objective self-analysis. One of the most helpful—and humbling—exercises I ever performed was an assignment given to us at Harvard called a "Self-Assessment and Career Development Paper." Basically, we were asked to generate data about ourselves by utilizing several professional assessment tools, report what these tools uncovered about our true strengths and weaknesses, and then develop a career plan that would benefit from our strengths. I went through twenty formal inventories and other exercises and then wrote a twenty-three-page paper that pretty clearly spelled out what I was good at, what I valued, and what I wasn't so good at.

Online Assessments

Regardless of where you are in your career, I strongly recommend that you engage in some type of formal assessment process to help you clearly identify your skills, interests, values, and personality type. Basically, there are two ways to do this: self-directed through online assessments or professionally administered through institutions such as a college or university, job-placement services, or career counseling services. Online assessments are either free or relatively inexpensive, but most career counselors consider this the least reliable way to get a clear picture of your strengths and weaknesses because they do not provide professional interpretation of the results. Some assessments are scaled-down, online versions of well-known, reputable inventories, and others are simple tests that are quick and fun but not necessarily accurate. However, if funds are tight and you take several of these tests to compare results and identify trends, it's a good place to start. Here are just a few of the more popular online inventories:

Campbell Interest and Skill Survey. This is the online version of a well-known and reputable assessment that contains 320 multiple-choice questions and provides a report comparing your results to people in careers that you are interested in. Cost: $18. (www.profiler.com/cgi-bin/ciss/moreform.pl?client=ncs&referrer=8page=index)

Career Direct Personality ID Survey. A relatively simple test to help you determine your personality type by having you rank sixteen sets of four descriptive words. Cost: free. (*www.careerdirectonline.org/personalityID/*)

Career Fit Test. This is a seventy-two-item assessment that helps you determine the type of workplace you would enjoy and in which you could be successful. Cost: $6. (http://careerfit-test.com/)

Career Liftoff Interest Inventory. This is a 240-question inventory that provides a detailed profile using popular codes developed by Dr. John Holland, a leader in career assessment. Both the profile and narrative reports are sent to you immediately after taking the online assessment. Cost: $19.95. (www.careerliftoff.com/)

Compass Report. A two-hundred-item assessment suited primarily for people thinking about changing careers or who want to assess how well they are suited for their current job. Cost: $39. (www.hoganassessments .com/compass)

Future Proof Your Career. Especially helpful for those who want to make sure their skills stay current with trends in a variety of careers. A detailed seven-page report is emailed to you after taking the assessment. Cost: free; an interpretive book is available for $29.95. (www.future-proofyourcareer.com/)

Kiersey Temperament Sorter. A 70-question survey related to the popular and reputable Myers-Briggs Type Indicator (MBTI). Cost: free for basic report, with additional reports available from $4.95 to $19.95. (http://keirsey.com/sorter/instruments2.aspx?partid=0)

Professional Assessments

The data you gain from these kinds of online assessments will be helpful, but the value of professionally administered assessments will give you a more in-depth look at your strengths and weaknesses. One of the best resources for this kind of career help is your college or university, since most will continue to provide assistance to you after you graduate. Also, your current employer's human resource department may also be a good place to receive professional assistance to determine your strengths and learn how to build on them to advance your career. Finally, you might also consider using a professional career-counseling or coaching service—the National Career Development Association provides a free service for finding certified career counselors in your area (http://associationdatabase.com/aws/NCDA/pt/sp/consumer_find).

Obviously you can spend a lot of time and money on professionally administered assessments, but I recommend you take at least one of the following:

Myers-Briggs Type Indicator (MBTI). Perhaps the granddaddy of them all, this test has been touted as "the most widely used personality assessment," with as many as two million assessments administered annually. In fact, many businesses use it with potential new hires. Based on your answers to 93 questions, you will be given a personality type expressed in combinations of letters representing qualities such as extraversion, introversion, sensing, intuition, and so on. Additionally, you will be asked to take the "Best Fit" exercise which will help you determine the types of work in which you would most likely excel.

StrengthsFinder 2.0 is an updated version of the popular assessment created by the late Donald O. Clifton, Tom Rath, and a team of scientists from Gallup. This popular book, available at most bookstores, provides an assessment that will identify your strengths and then provides strategies for applying those strengths to your career.

Strong Interest Inventory is another widely used assessment considered extremely reliable in determining which career or occupational choices would be best for you based on your interests. Developed in 1927 by E. K. Strong (thus the name), this test is designed to be administered by a professional who will then assist in interpreting the data. It's best for those who are either still in college (more than 70 percent of colleges use this test) or who have begun working but do not feel comfortable or satisfied with the type of work they are doing.

The Birkman Method. A popular personality test used by thousands of businesses to help their employees maximize their performance. The test is delivered online but is administered and interpreted by certified consultants who have been trained to work with individuals in using the information to build their careers. This assessment tends to be used more at the executive level, focusing on leadership and management positions.

On-the-Job Assessments

In addition to online and professionally administered assessments, you can also learn a lot about your strengths on the job. For example, most companies provide at least an annual performance review. Rather than dreading those events, I always looked forward to them because I received an honest, objective appraisal of my skills and abilities. Many companies also provide opportunities for their employees to participate in "360 degree" assessments or executive coaching that provide input from your superiors, your peers, and your subordinates.

Finally, there's still another way to get informal yet helpful feedback about your strengths, and that is to seek it out directly from a close, trusted colleague. In fact, in the January 2005 issue of the *Harvard Business Review*, management professors Laura Roberts and Gretchen Spreitzer and their colleagues propose a "Reflected Best Self" exercise, in which you actively solicit feedback from those who know you well. We all have them, right? Someone we work closely with, perhaps travel with from time to time. And we've developed a close enough relationship with them to know they will tell us the truth.

One time after I had been at IBM for over a year at one of its divisions' headquarters, my boss, Lee Sechler, and I were having a chat. I felt very comfortable with Lee and knew that he was a professional manager, so I decided to get his perspective on my performance.

"I have been in a professional role for over a year since I graduated from Oregon State, and I would like to get some candid feedback," I began. "What one thing would you suggest I focus on in order to have a better chance of success in my career?"

Lee didn't miss a beat and gave it to me straight.

"Diane, you are a competitive, goal-oriented person, but these strengths can also be a weakness. There are people you are going to work with who don't share those characteristics. You need to alter your expectations of others. You can be hard on people who you need to get things done so that you achieve the desired result for your division."

I remember his advice to this day and continue to work on that weakness.

The inclination for most of us is to get defensive about the negative comments we receive from these evaluations, but they are a great mirror for you to take a closer look at yourself and then act on the results. In fact, what was so helpful with my career development paper was taking all the data I received from the various tests and inventories and making some decisions that allowed me to build on my strengths.

Putting Your Strengths to Work

When my good friend Dan called me about possibly moving into the real-estate business by taking a job that was available at Trammell Crow, I hesitated because I just didn't think I was cut out for real estate. His response caught me up short.

"Diane, think about what makes you tick. You're very project oriented/results oriented. Pulling a team together and executing a plan. Working with people. Don't think so much about real estate, but about what you like to do and how this job will let you do that."

Wow! Here I was into my second job after getting my MBA and not really feeling all that fulfilled in my work, and he nailed it for me—showed me that you grow your career on your strengths, not so much on any particular business. I had it backward—I was looking for a great job with opportunities for career growth when I should have been looking first at what I did really well and what I liked doing. Once I found a "home" where I could apply my greatest strengths to my work, my career really took off.

Of course I did very well at my first two jobs, but just because you're getting good performance reviews doesn't mean you're in the right job. Based on what you have learned about your strengths, is your current job (or the direction you're heading) maximizing your strengths, or are you simply performing well in areas that do not really interest you? I realize that especially when you start out, you may have to take jobs that are not the best fit for you. But that should never stop you from looking for ways to better align your strengths and interests with your work.

That's exactly what Kathy did. Fresh out of college with a degree in business, Kathy signed on with a large advertising agency in Chicago to work in their finance department. She was good at what she did and received a promotion within six months, but the more she worked in the department, the more she knew it just wasn't for her. Fortunately, she had a sympathetic supervisor who recognized Kathy's talents and directed her to the human resources department, which began helping her determine her strengths and looking for other areas in the company where she might better use those strengths. Taking the Myers-Briggs test confirmed what she already knew — she was an extravert. But her HR colleague helped her see that as an extravert she would never be fulfilled working in finance, even though she received high marks there. Eventually, they found her a position where she worked with clients, managing their accounts and helping to solve their media needs. It wasn't long before she was made vice president, leading a team of creative professionals that benefited from her energetic and empathic leadership. It was a win for the company because they held on to a valuable employee, and it was a win for Kathy because, as she put it, "I absolutely love going to work every day."

That's what happens when you trade on your strengths.

For Reflection and Discussion

1. Make a list of ten skills or things that you do well. (Not just right now, but think back to when you were in junior high, high school, and college.) Then go back and circle two or three that you do extremely well. How do you use those two or three things in your current job?

116

2. In addition to your classes and major field of study in college, what other activities did you pursue because you had a strong interest in them (athletics, student government, clubs, etc.)? What was it about those activities that appealed to you? How could those interests translate into the type of work for which you would be best suited?

3. Reflect back on your most recent performance review. How much time was spent reviewing your strengths—your successes? How much on your weaknesses—your failures? In what ways could a performance review be an opportunity for you to trade more on your strengths at your company?

4. In order for you to advance in your company, will you be moving more in the direction of your strengths or more in the direction of your weaknesses? If a promotion meant that you would be doing things in which you had little interest or that did not maximize your strengths, what would you do? In conjunction with evaluating your strengths in a new role, have you considered your priorities in life and how the new opportunity fits with what you value most in your life?

5. What specific things will you do over the next six months to gain a clearer understanding of your strengths?

Focus on the Good

If your work doesn't let you do what you do best, you're not alone. In his book *Now, Discover Your Strengths*, Gallup researcher Marcus Buckingham refers to a massive survey of 1.7 million workers in 101 companies from sixty-three countries. When asked the question "At work, do you have the opportunity to do what you do best every day?" only 20 percent answered positively.

Buckingham believes companies would thrive if employees could do what they are really good at doing. But few companies and individuals even know what that is. "We don't look in the mirror very often because we're frightened we won't see very much," Buckingham says. "We're not that special. We're not that good. We're not that smart. It's the old imposter syndrome. But the fact is, we're all filled with naturally recurring patterns that make us unique — they're called talents. And our charge is to ... use them."[1]

Whether you are still in college, just starting out in your career, or several years with a company, ask yourself these three questions:

1. What are my greatest skills and qualities?
2. In what type of work setting can these be used most effectively?
3. In my current job, am I spending most of my time doing what I do best?

If there is a disconnect between the first two questions and the third one, it may be time to make some adjustments.

Where's the Passion?

Is it possible to find work that you are passionate about? Absolutely, but it may take some time and a willingness to move around a bit. Alan L. Sklover, a New York City attorney who represents executives, recommends against settling into a career too early. "Don't be afraid to take any job that interests you," he says. "You're not locked in for life. If there's one time you're supposed to take chances, it's while you're younger and relatively free of responsibilities. After that, trying something new takes courage that very few have." Sklover tells younger employees to try a variety of new jobs, keeping track of what they like and dislike about each job. "Sooner or later you'll develop a sense of direction—and maybe even a passion about what you do for a living."[2]

Here are some statements that help identify whether or not you are passionate about your career:

- Most days I am excited about going to work.
- I seldom find myself losing interest in a project or assignment.
- I enjoy the people with whom I work.
- I feel as if I am making a difference in my company.
- It's easy for me to "brag" about my company.
- I love my job.
- Even though it's called "work," most of the time it's fun.
- I'm always confident that I will succeed.
- I can't believe they pay me for this!

the facts
about faith

WE'VE ALL SEEN HER. She shows up for work every day driving a car with that bumper sticker: "Honk if you love Jesus!" Decked out in cross earrings and a cross necklace, she carries her briefcase in one hand and her Bible in the other. Her coffee mug has the name of her church emblazoned on it, and on the corner of her desk sits the ubiquitous miniature statue of Jesus washing Peter's feet. If you have any doubts about her beliefs, they completely disappear when you join her for lunch and she very deliberately bows her head, closes her eyes, and remains in that prayerful state for what seems like an eternity as you politely yet awkwardly wait for her to finish.

Then there's the other extreme. The late Bob Briner, a powerful sports media executive and author of a wonderful book *Roaring Lambs*, worked closely with a business associate for twenty years before, by chance, they both discovered each other was a Christian. Both had been so careful not to offend anyone at work with their beliefs that they pretty much kept their Christian faith locked up tightly in a private compartment of their lives, missing out on years of spiritual fellowship.

The dance we face as Christian professional women weaves somewhere between these two extremes. On the one hand, we want to honor God, not just in church on Sunday mornings but in all areas of our lives, including work. Ask any person who grew up in church who the light of the world is, and they'll quickly answer, "Jesus." They may have remembered an old chorus called "The Light of the World is Jesus." Or they correctly recall reading in the Bible where Jesus declared he was "the light of the world" (John 8:12). But their answer would only be half right, because in his one recorded sermon in the Bible, Jesus says to his followers, "You are the light of the world" (Matthew 5:14). This was his way of inviting us to share in his ministry of bringing hope and healing to the world, and I haven't found any place in the Bible that tells us we should do this everywhere but on the job. In fact, you probably will have no other place where you have as much of an opportunity to influence others toward God than in the workplace. And yet, living in a pluralistic and largely secular society, even unintentional gestures or expressions of faith can be offensive to others.

I've been trying to master that dance for more than twenty years and still occasionally find myself stumbling one way or the other. It's not easy. But I've come to some conclusions that serve as my guiding principles when it comes to faith in the workplace.

Principle #1— Be a Full-Time Christian

Faith isn't something you turn on and turn off. When you turn your life over to Christ, you belong to him and he lives in and through you. All the time. We sometimes talk about our "identity in Christ" as being transformed into a new person (2 Corinthians 5:17). It's *who* we are as much as it is *what* we are, for it defines our entire being. We don't give God only our spiritual selves when we surrender to him. We give him everything, and that includes our talents, our gifts, and yes, the part of us that goes to work every day.

Are there challenges involved in living out your faith in the work-place? Absolutely, and it will vary depending on the company you work for. Some, in fact, may have strict rules against any direct and outward display of any religious faith. But that doesn't mean we set aside our faith when we get in the elevator. Being a young woman in the workplace will place tremendous demands on your time, your energy, and even sometimes your core beliefs and morals. This is not the place to leave your faith at the door and try to go it alone, and the good news is that you don't have to.

Principle #2 — Remember Who You Work For

I fully believe that every good gift — even my job — comes from God. But not to sound crass, he doesn't sign my paycheck. Even though you're a full-time Christian, you have an ethical obligation to put in an honest day's work for the company that hired you. Well-intentioned efforts to use your job to "witness" to others about your faith violate that obligation. Most companies view overt efforts to proselytize or influence others toward any religion to be a huge distraction and therefore completely inappropriate. I totally agree. In fact, I would probably tell you — Christian to Christian — that the best way you can become a shining light for Christ is to be the best employee in the company (Colossians 3:23). When you're at work, you are there to serve your employer, but at the same time, when you are serving your employer well, you are serving God.

Does this mean you should never pray at work, read your Bible, or talk about a church missions trip you experienced? Of course not, but it's *how* you do those things. I probably couldn't make it through a day at work without praying, but you probably wouldn't know it because I'm careful not to make a big deal about it. I also know that if I have a lot of time to go around talking to my colleagues about my beliefs, I'm probably not delivering the goods for my company. Think about it for a second — what does it say about you to your colleagues if you aren't pulling your share of the weight in your office? Do you think they can respect the faith of a slacker?

Principle #3 — Respect Your Colleagues

Not everyone you work with is interested in your faith, and you need to respect that. Today's workplace is more diverse than at any other time in history. Not only are there more women in positions of leadership, but overall the workplace reflects the cultural, ethnic, and religious diversity of society at large. According to the American Religious Identification Survey the numbers of Muslims and Buddhists in America doubled from 1990 to 2008, while the number of Hindus has tripled. During the same period, the percentage of Christians in America dropped from 86 percent to 76 percent, and the percentage of those claiming no religious faith grew from 8 percent to 15 percent.[1] I'm not sure there ever was a time when you could expect that all the people you worked with believed as you did, but clearly today there's a good chance that the people in your department represent a variety of religious groups as well as those who are not interested in *anything* religious.

Here again, just because your colleague is a Hindu doesn't mean you have to hide the fact that you're a Christian. One of the blessings of diversity is that it has made the entire working environment more sensitive to the religious beliefs of all employees. Many larger companies are providing quiet rooms for Muslim employees and those of other faiths to pray, for example. Auto giant Ford Motor Company formed the Ford Interfaith Network to accommodate the religious needs of all its employees, which include Buddhists, Catholics, Mormons, evangelical Christians, Hindus, Muslims, Jews, and Eastern Orthodox Christians. The company even offers some of its facilities for after-hours use by religious groups.

Given this diverse and increasingly supportive environment for people of all religions, it is even more important to respect the beliefs of others as you live out your own faith. I love my friend Stacy Repult's "one cross rule." When she first mentioned it, I had no idea what she was talking about, so she explained: "If you show up for work wearing a cross necklace, cross earrings, a cross bracelet, and a cross pin on your lapel, that's way over the top and offensive to others. But one cross is fine."

Always remember that the person next to you may be as devoted to *her* faith as you are to yours. Respect that.

Principle #4 — Show, Don't Tell

When it comes to your faith, the way you live speaks louder than the words you use. Consider these wise words from St. Francis of Assisi: "Preach the gospel at all times — if necessary, use words." Or as my friend Frances Hesselbein says, "Live the example." (See sidebar on page 130.) That starts with being a good, honest employee. Too often that woman wearing all the crosses is also the one who is always trying to talk to colleagues about her faith while they're trying to get their work done. Unless I knew a colleague was a believer, I never deliberately went out of my way to talk with one about my faith. However, I *have* had people I work with say things privately to me, such as, "You're different — what makes you tick?" Or "How do you manage to stay calm with all this stress?" When your colleagues ask you questions like this, it's usually because they've been observing you for a while and are interested in learning more about you. Only then have you earned the right to speak directly about your faith.

One of my favorite Bible verses that speaks to this appears in Paul's letter to the Christians in the city of Philippi: "Do everything without complaining or arguing, so that you may become blameless and pure, children of God without fault in a crooked and depraved generation, in which you shine like stars in the universe" (Philippians 2:14–15). I'm certainly not blameless or without fault, but I've learned that if you let your faith guide you in all you do, you won't need to go around letting everyone know you're a Christian. They'll know.

Principle #5 — Look for Allies

I've had some great friends from the places I've worked who were wonderful Christians, and it was such a source of encouragement to be able to talk openly with them about our shared faith. One of my executive buddies at a particular firm would occasionally come into my office, and we would pray together for another C-level leader. In another company, a group of believers formed an informal email list where we would share prayer requests. And if I was having lunch with a colleague I knew was a believer, one of us would quietly say grace before we ate. These may seem like small things, but having a few good Christian friends at work is a real blessing.

How do you find them? The same way you hope they would find *you*: look for other "shining stars." I can't guarantee that every honest, hard working, compassionate, and friendly person at work is a Christian, because people of other faiths as well as people with no religious faith also can have strong, positive values. But that's a good place to start. Also, pay attention. I had a hunch that Craig, one of the guys I worked with, was a fellow believer just by watching him interact with people. But the real "tell" was when he casually mentioned that he was a trustee on the board of his church.

Principle #6 — Watch Your Language

Even if a colleague asks you one of those "wide open door" questions that invites you to talk about your faith, think before you speak. I'll never forget the time one of my colleagues in a meeting asked Don Williams, the chairman of Trammell Crow, what was important to him in life. I had known that Don was a strong believer who attended church regularly, so I was more than a little curious to hear his answer.

"My faith is at the core of my life," he began. "Faith and family are ahead of everything else."

He could have used that opportunity—along with the fact that he was everyone's boss—to preach a little mini-sermon: "I believe in Jesus, the only begotten Son of God who with God the Father and the Holy Spirit make up the Trinity. Yada yada yada."

But he didn't. What he said was enough. Just right. For any individual who was interested in learning more, I know he would have been glad to meet with them over lunch and explain his beliefs more explicitly. For those who couldn't care less, he spared them all that religious jargon that only other Christians understand.

Other Voices

Don also had another way of subtly sharing his faith at work that not only wasn't offensive to others but was actually helpful. He read widely and had a mind like a sponge, so he would often quote from a book he had read or share some principles he had learned in the book. Obviously, he always had the right quote or information that fit into whatever topic we might be discussing in a meeting. In addition to great material from writers like Jim Collins or Peter Drucker, he would occasionally include writers like Max Lucado or John Maxwell. Only those of us who were Christians knew that these were popular Christian authors—but they are also authors who have written extensively on leadership and motivation, so it made sense to include them on his list of recommended reading.

Sometimes it just makes sense to let others who are more qualified speak for us. In addition to referring colleagues to books (see "A Few Good Books" sidebar on page 130), you could also introduce your friends at work to inspirational recording artists, such as Steven Curtis Chapman, TobyMac, MercyMe, or Casting Crowns. And if a colleague expresses interest in talking with you about issues of faith and you feel, as I sometimes do, that you might not have all the right answers or know what to say, here's where your "allies" can be helpful: "Would you mind if Theresa joined us for lunch to talk about this? I'm kind of new at this God stuff, and she's helped me learn a lot."

A few years ago a young woman went to work for a large law office in Chicago. She immediately became friends with a woman a few years her senior, and over the course of two years, she began attending a church for the first time in her life.

"I was never really religious, and in college I got really turned off by the Christians who were always trying to save me," she recounted. "But

Amy was different. She never said anything to me about her beliefs and was just a fun person. When I got a phone call one day that my mom had suffered a stroke, I went immediately to her office, closed the door, and started to cry. I just needed a shoulder, and I knew she would understand. When I finally was able to tell her what had happened, she said something that just sounded so caring: 'Would you like me to pray for your mom?' If you had asked me what I thought about prayer, I would have told you it was for weak people who couldn't figure things out on their own, but right at that moment it made sense. She closed her eyes and said something real simple like, 'God, please be close to Jen's mom right now.' That was it. My mom recovered, but over the next few months, I took every chance I could get to ask Amy about her beliefs, and the next thing I knew, I was in church for the first time in my life and developing a personal relationship with Christ."

I don't know Amy—a friend shared this story with me. But I can almost bet she's never violated the one-cross rule. She didn't need to carry a sign that let everyone know she was a Christian. If we live out our faith in the workplace, we will never have to initiate a conversation about our love for God. Those who seek him will find him.

Through you.

For Reflection and Discussion

1. In your own faith journey, who were the people in your life that seemed to draw you toward a belief in God? What was it about them and their faith that made them appealing to you?

2. What are some of the negative attitudes toward Christianity that you have observed from your friends or colleagues? Why do you think people have these attitudes? What can you do to try to alter your behavior so that others in the workplace will feel open to approaching you about your faith?

3. Are you aware of other Christians in your company? If so, how do you know?

4. Have you approached Christians in your company so that you can support each other, support other employees, and pray about God's use of you in your workplace?
5. When it comes to faith in the workplace, every company is different. From your experiences, describe your company's compatibility with your faith. Is it a good place for a Christian to work? Is it hostile to Christianity? Explain. If it is a hostile place, do you feel that God has a reason for you to be there, or are you looking at finding a work environment that is more supportive of your faith?
6. In what ways are you "living the example"? How would your colleagues know about your faith?

A Few Good Books

Here's a sampling of books that are written from a faith-based perspective but appeal to virtually anyone because they do not use unfamiliar religious jargon or attempt to proselytize:

Facing Your Giants by Max Lucado. Bestselling inspirational author uses the familiar David and Goliath story to motivate those who have ever felt overpowered in life.

The 21 Irrefutable Laws of Leadership by John Maxwell. Internationally recognized leadership expert offers practical advice to help leaders at every level of an organization.

Integrity by Henry Cloud. Clinical psychologist and management consultant writing for business leaders.

Jesus, CEO by Laurie Beth Jones. Bestselling author and management consultant extracts practical leadership principles from the teachings of Jesus.

The Servant Leader by Ken Blanchard. Popular author of *The One Minute Manager* summarizes four dimensions of leadership.

The Purpose-Driven Life by Rick Warren. Practical, readable advice on finding meaning and purpose in life. More than 25 million sold.

Traveling Mercies by Anne Lamott. Bestselling author's spiritual memoir.

Share Your Faith at Work?

The way you live communicates volumes about what you believe. Here are a few ways to communicate the gospel at work without having to use too many words:

Strive to live out your faith in every part of your life, so it becomes an integral part of every ordinary encounter you have with people. Remember that this is how the first Christians lived. It was natural for them to share their faith with people in the marketplace and workplace.

Realize that the simple can be profound. Know that simple activities such as listening compassionately to a customer or sharing lunch with a colleague, can be powerful ways to plant seeds of faith in people's lives. Understand that God uses everything, no matter how insignificant it may seem to you.

Treat other people with consideration. Realize that people won't care how much you know until they know how much you care. Consistently show you care by avoiding gossip, pursuing honesty in all situations, and genuinely listening to others' concerns. Practice common courtesies on a regular basis.

Never force discussions about faith. Doing so does more harm than good. Keep in mind that mentioning faith is only appropriate when it arises naturally out of your relationships at work, when it naturally fits into the topic of conversation, or when someone asks you about your faith.

Don't try to do God's job. Don't try to take on the burden of convincing people of spiritual truths. Realize that only the Holy Spirit can transform someone's heart. Instead, seek simply to show others how God has made a difference in your life and can make a difference in theirs.

Don't be afraid to show your own flaws. Too many Christians try to seem perfect, only to come across as arrogant and phony. Remember that non-Christians will be attracted not by your victories but by God's grace. Know that they need to see not just who you are today, but where you've come from.

Invite people from work to share nonwork activities with you. Make time in your schedule to spend with non-Christians as well as Christians, remembering that doing so was important to Jesus himself. Pursue common interests with people from work—from playing on a sports team together to seeing a movie you both want to see. Let common needs draw you together, such as forming a carpool. Share your common gifts and talents; for instance, weekend musicians could start a band together. Connect with each other through your common concerns, such as parenting.[2]

Just Be Yourself

Hailey Robinson is earnest about building her career as a tax accountant without sacrificing her faith.

"It's easy to get sidetracked by our work, regardless of the industry you're in," she explains. "I start every day with devotions because if I don't, I get to work with a totally different mind-set that doesn't always reflect my faith. I want my colleagues to know I'm a Christian by how I act, not by what I say."

Robinson also attends a Bible study during the day every Wednesday but was straightforward with her manager about it.

"I told her this was a priority for me and that I could make up the time by working later that day. She was very supportive and encouraging to me."

When it comes to living out your faith in the workplace, Robinson advises others to simply be themselves and not try to force their beliefs on anyone.

"I don't try to hide the fact that I'm a Christian — it's not unusual for me to even mention something from the Bible in a conversation with a colleague. They know that my faith is a big part of who I am, but there are people from other faiths in my office and it wouldn't be appropriate to debate them or try to convert them. The neat thing is that every now and then a colleague will approach me with questions about faith, and that always results in some great conversations."

what about church?

As someone who grew up in church and has benefited from all the church has to offer, I can't imagine growing in my faith without being part of a dynamic church. My little church in Harrisburg gave me the foundation that allowed my faith to flourish when I got to college, as well as a great group of Christian friends, which probably kept all of us from getting into too much trouble during my teenage years.

There's another reason church is so important to me. When I was six months old, I was diagnosed with spinal meningitis and wasn't given a great chance of surviving. My mom and dad asked the church and our preacher to pray over me. I honestly believe I am alive today because the people in my little church prayed for my healing. My brother and mom remind me that God must have spared me because he had a plan for me, and that helping young professional women who are serious about Christ may be a part of his plan.

Unlike a lot of churched kids who take a break from church during their college years, I couldn't wait to attend the Gathering every week — a student-led ministry that served the purpose of a church and really ignited my faith. Throughout all my moves—even during my two years at Harvard—I always looked for a church and tried to attend as often as I could.

Not that it's always been an enriching experience. Once I got rolling in my career, more often than not when I went to church it felt like I didn't quite fit in. Many of my friends, still single and working, felt the people of the church seemed to think the greatest spiritual need in their lives was to get married. Their "singles' class" was basically eharmony. com offline, and all the well-meaning comments from the dear ladies who couldn't believe they went to college and failed to get their Mrs. degree only made them feel even more out of place.

Even after I met the unwritten requirement that I had to have a husband before I could be treated like a *real* adult woman, I still felt like the new kid in school that no one would play with when I went to church. It's not that no one tried. Church people are some of the nicest people in the world, and in many ways they bent over backward to welcome me whenever I started attending a new church. It's just that churches generally organize around categories, and few churches had a category for me: a young professional woman trying to balance the three loves of her life—faith, family, and career.

If society is finally getting comfortable with young, successful career women, the church is still trying to figure out what to do with us. I've been at this for a long time now, and I've yet to find a church that addresses the specific needs of a professional Christian woman.

Weekly Women's Coffee Hour

You have probably picked up by now that I'm not really a feminist in the classic, political sense of that term. I don't have an axe to grind about inequities that women still face, and I don't have to see a woman preaching in my church to feel respected and affirmed as a woman. In reality, I'm a fairly conservative woman who enjoys her career, likes being a mom and wife, and goes to church regularly. What could be so hard about that?

Plenty.

I hope your church is different, and I'm sure more churches are doing a better job serving people like us. But take a look at the special events and services most churches offer women. One of the most popular—and for good reason—is a weekly coffee hour/Bible study. Perfect combination, if you ask me. Coffee. A roomful of women. And the Bible. I'd love to be a part of something like that, but I can't because they always seem to be at 10:00 a.m. on Thursdays. You know where I am at 10:00 a.m. on Thursdays, and every other day of the week? At my desk. Or in a conference room. Or racing to catch a plane.

You know what I'm talking about.

Just for fun, I went to the website of a large church in another city that I know is a dynamic and positive presence there. The kind of church I would be attracted to and I'm sure you would be too. I navigated through their excellent website and found a Bible study for women between the ages of twenty-one and thirty. When do you think it met? Nine thirty. In the morning! If you're a young professional Christian woman, you're left out when it comes to that women's Bible study. I'm sure that church had no intention of ignoring your needs, but in essence they were saying, "If you want to grow in your faith here, quit your day job."

Then I went to another church's website—one that is known for being contemporary and whose pastor is well known from the books he's written. It was in an upscale suburb of a large city and like most churches provides separate, dynamic ministries for men and for women. But for some reason, the women's regular weekly meeting runs from 7:00 to 8:00 in the evening while the men meet from 5:30 to 6:30 in the morning. I guess they think only the men have to be to work by 8:00 or that women don't mind rushing home from work at 5:30 to put a meal on the table and then rush off to their women's meeting while their husbands help the kids with their math.

If I were writing this in longhand, I'd put one of those little smiley faces at the end of that last sentence to let you know I'm really just having some fun and not trying to bash churches.

But these examples underscore the reality that even some of the most forward-thinking churches don't really have women like us on their radar screens. I'm not advocating that we take over the place, but why are the men asked to serve on building committees and finance committees while the women are invited to work in the nursery or plan the next church potluck? I recently learned about a church locked in a dispute with the city zoning board. They turned it over to the chairman of the facilities committee to handle (a retired science teacher), despite having three young women in the church who were attorneys—one with a firm that routinely resolved similar disputes for private citizens.

Churches like these aren't opposed to women in leadership, nor do they deliberately try to keep women out of positions of responsibility. It's like muscle memory—when it comes to the heavy lifting, they think men. When it comes to more domestic tasks, they think women.

Feel Like Giving Up?

Unfortunately, a lot of young professional women check out a church, discover it really doesn't have much for them, and then leave. And pretty much never go back ... to any church. According to LifeWay Research, 70 percent of 21–30-year-olds who attended church in high school quit attending sometime between the ages of 18–22. The largest percentage (27 percent) left because of moving away to college, but 20 percent said they left because they didn't feel connected to the people in their church, and 7 percent said they did not feel involved in meaningful work at the church.[1] I know this survey included women *and* men, but it confirms my own observations that too many young professional women give up on church.

In her book *Quitting Church*, Julia Duin, a reporter for the *Washington Times*, refers to research that shows women and singles are leaving evangelical churches in ever-increasing numbers. One of the reasons echoes my own experience in that they don't really know what to do with us. According to Duin, women leave their churches because they are asked to do too little; their gifts and talents are not being used by their churches.[2] Duin knows firsthand what it's like to be a young professional woman marginalized by her church—she left her church in 2001 and didn't find one that met her needs until 2007. As a young professional journalist, she just didn't fit.

Maybe it's because I'm naturally a problem solver, but despite the fact that you might feel like an alien when you go to church, quitting isn't the answer. Sometimes at work I still run into some of that "good old boys" thinking and even outright resentment that I'm in a position of executive leadership, but so what? Would I quit a job I love just because of a few obstacles? I've always felt the same way about church. Despite not quite fitting in, I love the church and believe being part of a healthy church is an integral component of a vibrant Christian life. I would hate to think of going through some of the difficulties I've faced if I hadn't belonged to a church. There's too much to gain from regularly worshipping with others, learning from good preaching, being lifted up through inspiring music, and developing new friendships. Even if you don't always feel as if the church understands you, it provides a spiritual home that we all need to grow in our faith.

So if quitting isn't an option, what do you do? How do you, as a young professional Christian woman, deal with the whole church issue? In all fairness, I'm sure there are a number of churches that get it, even though I haven't found one yet. But as I've begun working with other young professionals, I'm learning that if you look hard enough you will find a church that understands your needs and provides ministry and service opportunities that benefit from your talents and skills. If you've tried church and it doesn't feel right for you, it's perfectly okay to leave—but don't give up on church entirely. Keep looking. Especially if you live in or near a major city, you will likely find a church that understands the needs of young professional women.

For example, Redeemer Presbyterian Church in New York City not only seeks out and welcomes young professional women, they provide small groups based on various professions rather than personal interests such as parenting, homemaking, etc. I would have loved to have found a church that offered small groups in these areas that Redeemer provides: advertising professionals, business professionals, finance professionals, entrepreneurs, lawyers, health-care professionals, actors, and educators.[3] Across town, Trinity Church Wall Street also gets it and provides a lunch-hour Bible study specifically for professionals working on Wall Street.

You might expect the eleven thousand churches affiliated with the Willow Creek Association (www.willowcreek.com) would understand your needs; founder and successful pastor Bill Hybels has always had a heart for business and leadership. Willow Creek's annual Leadership Summit almost always includes prominent women CEOs such as Hewlett-Packard's Carly Fiorina on the platform alongside successful leaders like Jim Collins, Jack Welch, and Tony Blair. They clearly get it, and their website provides a search function to help you find one of their churches near you.

In fact, before the internet, if you wanted to check out a church you pretty much had to visit it and determine if it was right for you. Now you can google churches in your city and click your way through websites to look for clues about how you might fit in. Just for fun, I tried this for Dallas and found a church not too far from where I live. I pulled up its homepage and immediately felt it had a contemporary look about it, so I started navigating. I read its mission and values statements and they seemed compatible with how I believe. Next, I checked out its governance and wasn't surprised to see all the elders were men, which usually means it has a fairly traditional view of women, at least in *church* leadership. I can handle that. So I clicked on its Staff button and was surprised to see they actually have a "pastor for women's ministries." So far, so good. Then I clicked on their Connect button, which took me to a page listing all of their small groups. In addition to the usual, the one that caught my eye described its target as "women from a variety of careers." Never mind that they also offered six early-morning weekly Bible studies for men. At least they have women like me on their radar screen, and that's better than most churches. If I didn't like my own church so well, based on my surfing, I would probably at least have paid them a visit.

In the previous chapter, I suggested you try to connect with other believers at work, and they can be another source for finding a church that understands the needs of professional women. Just ask. In fact, that could also be a way to find other believers, as there's nothing threatening or offensive about asking, "I'm new in this area and looking for a church—do you go to church anywhere or know anyone who does?"

Use Your Entrepreneurial Spirit

Maybe you've tried dozens of churches and you still haven't found one that fits. You did the internet search, sought recommendations from your friends at work—nothing. It could happen. In fact, it's probably more likely to happen than not. You just happen to be one of those demographics that a lot of churches aren't prepared for, but why should that stop you from going to church? Why not face this challenge the same way you face challenges in your career: fix it!

Most of us got where we are in our careers because we're reasonably intelligent and know how to get things done. We fit that description that just about any professional job posting lists: self-starter. So why not use those skills to start your own professional women's ministry at your church? In fairness to churches, most of them really *don't* know what to do with young professional women, but that doesn't mean they don't care or don't *want* to meet their needs. I don't know of too many pastors who wouldn't be thrilled if someone approached them and offered to start a new ministry that would attract and retain people in their churches. Just be patient and persistent.

If possible, find one or two other women who share your concern and ask to meet with your pastor. Explain that you believe the church would benefit by reaching out to young professional women. Be positive. Don't complain that the church isn't doing much for you. Instead, help your pastor grasp your vision. Also, have a specific plan, even if it's as simple as putting an announcement on the church's website for a weekly meeting at a local coffee shop.

Focus on the Good

Sometimes, we are so focused on having our "niche needs" met that we miss out on all the good we can derive from belonging to a church. As much as I enjoy living in a country where you pretty much can get what you want, I wonder if that hasn't conditioned us as Christians to focus only on our specific needs. Does my church have a special ministry for senior executives who are women? No, but I'm part of a wonderful Sunday school class composed of couples like Chris and me. Some of the wives enjoy careers like mine, but many are stay-at-home moms. Being a part of this class has deepened my faith, strengthened our marriage, and helped us become better parents.

When I walk out of the church every Sunday morning, I always feel as if I have been fed. The preaching opens God's Word so clearly and shows me how to live it at home and on the job. When we sing as a congregation, my spirit soars as I worship God alongside other busy people trying to make it in a crazy world. I *need* my church. It gives me the strength to begin another week and the resolve to carry my faith with me into the marketplace.

As you look for that church where you will fit, don't ignore the good things it has to offer. A pretty good church is far better than no church at all.

For Reflection and Discussion

1. How would you rate your current church experience? What do you like about your church? What's missing that would make it a better fit?
2. If there was a time when you were a single adult and attending church, what was it like? Describe the singles' ministry at your church. How did other women who were married relate to you?

3. Have you ever stopped attending a church? What was it that led you to quit?

4. As a young professional Christian woman, what spiritual needs do you have that you think might be unique to you? What issues do you face that a stay-at-home mom or an older career woman might not face?

5. What's the one thing you wish a church would do for you as a young professional woman? Why is this so important to you? Have you ever expressed this to a pastor or church leader? If so, what happened? If not and you are attending a church, seek an appointment with your pastor to discuss this.

6. What could *you* do to address the needs of young professional women in your church?

Why You Need Church

Collette Chambers could not imagine skipping church. Not only does she regularly attend her home church in Washington, D.C., but she looks for churches to attend when she travels.

"I discovered Tokyo Baptist Church when I had to be in Japan on business," she laughs.

Chambers manages large integrated complex systems as an executive project manager for IBM. Her job takes her all over the world and like most executive positions, places demands on her personal life.

"Being part of a church nurtures my relationship with Jesus," Chambers explains. "It is where I learn sound doctrine and grow from my fellowship with others. They don't all have to be exactly like you. In fact, that's what makes church so interesting. It's where I perfect my people skills. It's integral to have a relationship with Christ so that I know how to relate to people."

Chambers considers her career — which includes stints at EDS, MIT, and the American Red Cross — as a ministry. She seeks out younger employees who seem to be struggling and invites them to come to her with their problems, which often opens doors for her to share her faith.

"I'm called to make an impact, and the best way I can do that is through everything God has given me — my talents, my skills, and my job. When you are given a talent and use it effectively for God, he multiplies it."

Her advice to young professional women who feel they can manage without being part of a church?

"Find a good church and get involved. You need a foundation—a rock. You need the sound teaching that attending church provides. Without it, your faith will falter."

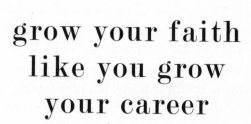

grow your faith like you grow your career

IN OUR EFFORTS TO BALANCE FAITH, family, and career, faith almost always takes a backseat. A typical day goes something like this:

Every morning I get up early, lace up my running shoes, and head out the door for my daily run. About forty-five minutes later it's time for a quick shower, and then I make sure the kids are up, fed, and off to school, with me not far behind on my morning commute. At work, I hit the ground running—meetings, phone calls, review reports, more meetings, problem solving, and at least one more impromptu meeting. I look at the clock and can hardly believe it's five thirty, so off I go to get dinner on the table and then preside over the randomness of having a house full of teenagers—my own kids and their friends—before Chris and I get a little time to ourselves. I look at my Bible on the nightstand next to my bed and tell myself now would be a good time to get caught up on my Bible Study Fellowship assignment. But I'm tired. I really should look over my presentation notes for tomorrow's budget meeting. I've had this article I've been wanting to read for a week. Annie is home from college and wants to hang out. I'm tired. I'm behind on my email. When was the last time Chris and I watched a movie together? I'm tired.

Finally, the weekend rolls around and I'm ready for it. I love my job, but it's been one of those weeks and I think you know what I mean. I'm looking forward to doing absolutely nothing except for joining a few other couples Saturday evening for dinner and fun. We get in pretty late, but it was worth it. Besides, I'm so looking forward to just chilling on Sunday. Going to church shouldn't be my only place for a quiet time with God, right? Maybe I'll use some of the time during the service to get caught up on my Bible Study Fellowship assignment.

Maybe not.

I've never met anyone who deliberately falls away from a dynamic and vibrant faith in God. Rather, it's a little like gaining weight. Those extra fifteen pounds don't just suddenly appear overnight but are the result of daily decisions over time that gradually rob you of your waistline. Likewise, our busy lives gradually crowd out those things that are essential to maintaining a personal relationship with God. According to the Barna Research Group, 34 percent of the Christian parents surveyed said that having enough time to devote to their faith was a major challenge.[1] I haven't done a formal survey, but among my friends who are professional Christian women, it's more like 99 percent. You can't let your job slide, and you try hard not to neglect your kids and spouse. The one area where we're most likely to take shortcuts, or that we may ignore outright, is our faith.

Why Bother?

One of the reasons I run every day is that running for me has become what physician and author William Glasser calls a "positive addition." Despite the effort and discipline it sometimes takes to get out the front door and start moving, running produces benefits—physical as well as emotional—that I have come to depend on. If for some reason I have to skip a few workouts, I miss those benefits: higher energy levels, more weight control, better ability to handle stress, stronger emotional health, and so on. I work out every day because overall it makes me feel better.

Our spiritual health ought to be more important than our physical health, and it requires the same kind of investment of our time. When you take the time to pray, read the Bible, and otherwise invest in the things of God, you feel closer to him, you have a confidence that he is with you, and you are able to view your life from a higher, wider perspective. Neglect it, and you begin to lose those benefits.

In her book *Listening for God*, Marilyn Hontz refers to those times when we do not actively pursue our relationship with Jesus as dry times. What an accurate image of what it's like to neglect our spiritual health. When I am closest to God—when I spend time regularly in his Word and set aside time each day to pray and listen for his voice—it's like dipping my hand into a crystal-clear mountain stream and drinking from it. But when I let the busyness of my life crowd into those times set aside for God, all that's left is the stagnant streambed. Ironically, it's when we are at our busiest that we need God's comforting presence the most.

When Trammell Crow Company was sold to CB Richard Ellis, the leadership asked me to run the business that served our corporate clients who outsourced its real-estate services. I was put in charge of pulling together 4,500 employees and over 300 clients into a cohesive leadership team with the goal of serving clients well with coordinated processes and a platform that took the best from both companies. The stress was incredible, but one of the things that got me through it was my personal morning prayer time that I combined with my morning run. It gave me incredible strength and kept me focused on the important things during this stressful period in my life.

And during one of the lowest times in my life, I don't think I could have survived without my faith. Sensing that our marriage was in serious trouble and heading for divorce, I would wait for my husband to come home—which was usually very late—so that the kids had someone in the house while they were asleep, then I would drive down to a pretty area with trees close to my house and read my Bible, pray, and meditate. Despite what was going on in my personal life, I felt so close to God. He gave me strength and showed me how to deal with this heartbreaking situation.

I'm far from perfect and have experienced my share of the dry times, but when my faith is strong and I am closest to God, the benefits spill over into my family and my work. I am a better parent, better spouse, and better worker when I put God first.

Spiritual Disciplines

More than thirty years ago, noted scholar and theologian Richard Foster wrote *Celebration of Discipline*, which immediately became a bestseller and continues to be a popular book for those who desire a deeper life of faith. Essentially, his book was a modern approach to what have been called the "classic spiritual disciplines," such as prayer, meditation, fasting, submission, service, and worship. But what makes this book so unique is the emphasis on celebration when it comes to discipline. Too many of us look at discipline from a negative point of view — it suggests a sense of obligation that pushes us to do something that we probably won't enjoy but it will be good for us. It's a loathsome means to an end: I hate doing these ab crunches, but if I keep at it, I won't be embarrassed to go in the hot tub at the ranch.

If you look at your spiritual growth that way, you'll always be tempted to skip that time you've set aside to pray or read your Bible or meditate. Two things will help. First, choose an activity or practice that fits who you are. Because I tend to be process oriented, I thrive on the systematic Bible studies produced by organizations such as Bible Study Fellowship (www.bsfinternational.org). I no longer look at my devotions as an obligation, but something I really look forward to. You may be wired differently and prefer something less structured. I know people who pray and meditate "on the run" during their daily workout. I have other friends who use their daily commute to listen to inspirational books that they've downloaded on their iPods. There's no real right or wrong way to practice your daily devotions; the important thing is to find a user-friendly way to connect with God on a daily basis.

The second way to turn your daily discipline into a positive addiction is to give it a chance. Remember when you decided to take up running? After that first run you felt pretty good, but the next day your muscles told you running wasn't such a good idea. But if you kept at it, you reached a point where you ran free of pain, learned how to pace yourself properly, and eventually arrived at that exhilarating place where you couldn't imagine *not* running.

Even if you really enjoy getting up half an hour early to read your Bible and meditate, you still need to give it time to become a habit. I've heard the oft-repeated claim that it takes twenty-one days to turn a helpful activity into a habit, but the only research I've seen on this suggests it takes more like sixty days.[2] It's probably different for everyone, but my point is that you need to select something you enjoy and then stick with it — probably for at least a month — before it becomes ingrained in your daily schedule.

Faith Training

Sometimes we make spiritual growth more complicated than it needs to be. Or we look for quick-fix formulas or a few easy steps and are disappointed when they don't deliver. Spiritual growth requires commitment, but it doesn't have to be difficult. When it comes to finding ways to supplement your daily devotions in order to grow stronger and deeper in your faith, consider the kinds of things you do to grow in your career.

Formal Training

You studied to prepare for a career, obtaining an undergraduate and possibly a graduate degree that provided a solid foundation upon which to build your career. The spiritual equivalent to this is the kind of consistent, systematic learning that you get by being part of a church (see previous chapter). Even if a church doesn't meet all of your needs as a young professional woman, it gives you a foundation of regular worship and biblical preaching that is necessary to a growing and dynamic faith. Many liturgical and mainline (Methodist, Presbyterian) churches base their Sunday worship on a lectionary, which is a systematic schedule of teaching the entire Bible from beginning to end. Most evangelical churches approach teaching more topically, yet still providing in-depth teaching from the Bible as it applies to contemporary life. Either way, you benefit spiritually from the specialized training of pastors who unpack the wisdom of God's Word, much as you gained from your professors in college.

Seminars and Workshops

Often in your career you will continue your professional development by attending seminars or workshops, usually offered at an industry-wide trade show. It's a great way to get specialized, up-to-date training that keeps you current in your particular field. After I graduated from Harvard Business School, some of my close friends attended the Foundation, a gathering of Christian business leaders founded by Bob Buford, and invited me to join them. For six years after graduate school, I had the chance to be around fellow Christian business leaders and be inspired by great music, amazing speakers, and deep fellowship.

In recent years, various Christian organizations have begun sponsoring national events that combine high-octane music and worship with dozens of focused seminars covering a wide range of topics relevant to today's Christian professional. I highly recommend you check out and consider attending the following:

The Catalyst Conference (www.catalystconference.com/) is billed as "the largest gathering of young leaders in the country" and "pure leadership adrenaline." Past speakers have included bestselling author Seth Godin, UN Human Rights Prize recipient Rani Hong, and Teach for America executive Nicole Baker Fulgham.

Willow Creek's Global Leadership Summit (www.willowcreek.com/events/leadership/2010/index.asp) is an annual event in August that brings together leaders from business, entertainment, government, and the church to address issues of leadership.

Urbana (http://www.urbana.org) is held every three years on the campus of the University of Illinois, with a special focus on helping young leaders from all walks of life understand how to use their careers for ministry. The event is sponsored by Inter-Varsity Christian Fellowship.

Small Groups

One of the side benefits of the team approach to business is that by bringing people together from different divisions in a company, you learn from one another. My main area of expertise is operations, but by working alongside team members from marketing, sales, finance, etc., I gained a wealth of knowledge that has helped me grow in my career. This is why I'm such a proponent of small groups as a way to grow in your faith and have tried to find time recently for Bible Study Fellowship. When you join a few others to study the Bible or an inspirational book together, or just meet to pray for each other and talk about your faith journeys, you gain new insights from their experiences that you would not arrive at on your own. Most churches offer small groups, but if you can't find one that suits you, put that entrepreneurial spirit to work and start your own. Between your contacts at work, Facebook, LinkedIn, MySpace, Twitter, etc., you ought to have no problem finding a few like-minded Christians who would enjoy participating in a small group with you.

Chris and I have been fortunate to be a part of a very close-knit group that meets Sunday mornings at our church. I have learned so much from the class discussion format of our group, plus, we are very close. In addition, one of my classmates from HBS, Vaughn Brock, kept encouraging me to start an accountability group with a group of senior Christian businesswomen. I did that two years ago with four special friends, and we have been there for each other ever since, even though our group is taking a break now. It took me a few years to act on Vaughn's urging; however, I am so glad I did.

Networking

I'm not sure where I would be without my network of friends and colleagues going all the way back to my undergraduate days. I'm pretty sure I wouldn't be where I am today, and I probably wouldn't have advanced as quickly in my career without that network. But I also have a network of Christian friends whom I can call anytime—day or night—for support. None of these friends attend the same church as I do and most don't live near me. In fact, if you're not fully connected to a church, it's even more important that you maintain a network of close Christian friends. These friends are from many parts of my life: neighbors in New Jersey, classmates from Oregon State and Harvard, friends from my church in Oklahoma, coworkers from Trammell Crow Company, businesswomen in Dallas, and even special friends I made on airplane flights. As the Nationwide insurance commercial used to say, "Life comes at you fast." There will be times when you need to be able to pick up your phone and call one of those special people who will listen and care and lift you up in prayer throughout your time of need. Social networks on the internet have their place, but in this case I'm talking about face-to-face friends you've made over the years.

Here in Dallas, Kat Armstrong and Stephanie Giddens started Polish, a wonderful outreach group for young professional women. Their organization hosts lunches that welcome women interested in learning more about the Christian faith, and networking opportunities offer advice on how to combine work with faith. It is the perfect example of a venue supporting and creating value for Christian businesswomen. After initially using Facebook as their marketing tool, today they have about sixty women on average attend lunch to connect with women in similar life stages and to absorb counsel from remarkable speakers every other Wednesday

Retreats

Nothing beats getting away for a couple of days in a nice environment with my leadership team to do some long-range planning or focus on a specific challenge. In a way, this book is a product of just such a retreat. I attended a Halftime seminar sponsored by Bob Buford, the author of the book with the same name. It challenged me to align my gifts with my passion for helping young professional Christian women.

In 2001, Chris and I decided one of the best vacations we could take with our new blended family was to attend Trail West, a Young Life Family Camp. Not only did our kids love it, so did we. It was great to spend a vacation filled with fun with other families focused on Christ as the center of their life.

Getting out of the office, away from interruptions, and into a comfortable setting really stimulates the creative juices and produces great results. Consider joining a women's or couples' retreat that most churches sponsor, or create your own personal spiritual retreat. Most states have several retreat centers that provide either guided spiritual retreats or allow you to design your own private retreat.

Online Training

The internet makes it possible for employees to upgrade their skills or gain new knowledge through specialized courses. This is yet another way to grow your faith. Protestant websites tend to focus more on devotionals and Bible studies, while Catholic sites usually feature spiritual formation classes, often guided by a spiritual director. One caution: "spiritual" resources on the internet can range from the legitimate to the loony. Always look for resources that are affiliated with trustworthy people or organizations. If you're not sure, consult your pastor or other Christian friends. Here are some organizations that can offer daily devotions, spiritual direction, or other resources:

www.crosswalk.com/devotionals/
http://odb.org/
www.upperroom.org/devotional/
http://utmost.org/
www.catholicspiritualdirection.org/csfsignup.html

www.henrinouwen.org/programs/spiritualdirection/main/
www.renovare.us/

Your Solid Rock

If you haven't discovered this already, you will: there's precious little that you really control in your life. You can do everything right at work, but find yourself on the wrong end of a merger that resulted in your entire department being eliminated. You can be the best mom on the planet and yet watch your children make poor choices that will break your heart. I experienced it. And sadly, despite working hard at your marriage, you might go through a divorce or separation.

What else have I got for you, right?

There's an old hymn that goes something like this: "On Christ, the solid Rock, I stand; all other ground is sinking sand." It was a somewhat homely musical rendition of a warning from Jesus as he concluded his Sermon on the Mount by essentially saying, "If you have listened to my words and put them into practice in your life, you will be like the man who built his home on the rock. When the rains came, his house stood firm. But if you heard these words and do not apply them to your life, you will be like the man who built his house on the sand. When the rains came, his house was swept away" (Matthew 7:24–27, author paraphrase).

Trust me, you'll experience a lot of rain in your family and career. Major thunderstorms, in fact. Distressing things will happen over which you have absolutely no control, but how you survive those storms depends on the one thing you *can* control: your relationship with God. He has given us his Word which teaches us how to live successfully, but we have to read it. He has invited us to talk to him and receive his guidance and comfort, but we have to find time in our busy lives for that. And he has given us the gift of his church and dedicated servants who want to help us grow in our faith. Ignore all of this, and our houses are built on sand.

I recall hearing about a middle-aged couple driving to a restaurant for a nice dinner together. About halfway to their destination, the wife wistfully asked, "Do you remember when we used to go on a date and I'd be snuggled in next to you as you cradled your arm over my shoulder?"

"Who moved?" he responded.

If you're feeling distant from God, maybe you just need to look over your shoulder and see that he's right there beside you. Where he's always been. And he wants nothing more than to walk with you closely.

It's how we grow.

For Reflection and Discussion

1. What are your biggest challenges to maintaining a strong, dynamic faith?
2. What types of activities do you try to engage in as a way of growing your faith?
3. Do you agree that when it comes to faith, family, and career, faith usually is the easiest to ignore? Explain.
4. Have you experienced any "storms" in your life so far? If so, what kinds of things helped you weather those storms?
5. When you hear the word *discipline*, what do you think? Do you consider yourself to be a person who enjoys or appreciates discipline? Can you identify an accomplishment or achievement in your life that came about primarily through discipline?
6. Identify four close friends with a strong faith that you can form a once-a-month meeting time over lunch to support each other.

Spiritual Growth Self-Test

1. I spend time daily in some form of devotional activity: prayer, Bible reading, meditating, etc.
2. I belong to a small group whose purpose includes spiritual growth.
3. I attend church regularly.
4. I have attended some type of spiritual retreat in the past year.
5. I have read at least one book in the past year whose topic dealt specifically with some aspect of the Christian life.
6. I have at least one or two close Christian friends who I trust enough to share my spiritual struggles with them or ask them to pray for me during a difficult time.

If you answered no to more than two of these questions and feel as if you are going through a "dry time" in your faith journey, consider ways to turn at least one of your no answers to a yes.

when you're both wearing the pants

I FEEL AS IF I'VE CHEATED YOU. We've gotten this far without exchanging recipes. I mean, come on. We're women, and we just *love* to cook, right? Actually, I do. Like they say, "You can take the girl out of the country, but you can't take the country out of the girl." I'm not saying I'm the *greatest* cook in the world, but my mom was, and growing up on the farm must have rubbed off on me, so here goes:

1 wife, approximately thirty years of age
1 husband of similar vintage
2 careers
Double wife's income and mix thoroughly
Caution: mixture could be volatile!

Okay, maybe a little cheesy, but you get the point. Trying to blend two personalities into a marriage is hard enough, but when both work— and especially when the wife earns more than her husband—you've got a potential disaster on your hands. Or a beautiful relationship that benefits from both of you working hard and earning a comfortable standard of living.

I'm pretty sure I know which one you want.

In my parents' and grandparents' generations, most women stayed home while the husband went off to work. In fact, up until the late 1970s, men and women had distinctly different roles which tended to form their identities—women were nurturers who pretty much ran the home while men were hunter-gatherers who provided the means for the family to survive. If you want to see a perfect example of this, go to YouTube and check out *Ozzie and Harriet*. One of the most popular television shows in the 1960s, it depicted the typical American family where Ozzie got a kiss from his wife, Harriet, as he walked out the door every morning to work while she stayed home to care for David and Ricky. They never fought because, well, it was television and the script writers never let them fight. But they also didn't have anything to fight over. He had his world, she had hers, and as long as they maintained those boundaries, everything was fine.

Fast forward to *your* world. According to historian Stephanie Coontz, marriage has changed more in the past thirty years than it has in the previous three thousand years.[1] The year 2009 marked the first time in history that the number of women in the workforce in the United States outnumbered men in the United States. Mothers today are either the primary breadwinners or co-breadwinners in nearly two-thirds of American families.[2] As recently as thirty years ago, dual-income marriages were the exception. In 1995, close to 61 percent of all married couples in the United States are dual income earners (higher in couples without children), and the percentage of marriages where the wife is the only breadwinner is increasing.[3] In 1970, only 37 percent of college-educated men were married to women who also had college degrees. Today, the number of college-educated men married to college-educated women has jumped to 71 percent.[4] Thanks to pioneering women who fought the gender battles in the sixties and seventies, we have the freedom to choose whether we want to stay at home or go to work, and the majority of us are choosing to go to work.

Like any cultural shift, the increase in dual-income marriages creates a new set of challenges for couples already trying to negotiate the intricacies of becoming "one flesh," primarily in the areas of money and roles. If you're a successful single woman and get married to a guy with a decent job, who handles the money? Since no one is home all day to do laundry, wash windows, and make dinner, who does those things and why? If your career flourishes with promotions and salary increases, and his doesn't, how do you keep that from interfering with your relationship? What do you do if he wants to start a family and also wants you to set your career aside temporarily to care for your child? Do you have separate or joint bank accounts? Credit cards? Investments?

Your grandparents had their own set of issues, but most likely never had to answer questions like these. And you better answer them, because ignoring them is absolutely the worst thing you can do and will only make matters worse. According to noted financial author Larry Burkett, "Money is either the best or the worst area of communication in our marriages." Unfortunately, most marriages tend to make it the worst, according to bestselling author Dave Ramsey: "After years as a financial counselor and working with marriage counselors, I know that money and money fights are a major cause of divorce, not to mention the thing we fight about the most."[5]

This Shouldn't Be So Difficult

To any of their family and friends, Tom and Angela had a storybook marriage. Both landed great jobs right after college, about two years before they got married, his with a Fortune 100 company, hers with one of the top law firms in their city. Unlike most young couples, they were able to buy a nice home in a quiet neighborhood thanks to two significant salaries. But almost from the beginning, they began to argue—usually over little things. For example, Tom had grown up in a traditional home where his dad worked and his mom stayed home even though she had a college degree. In that environment, he had grown accustomed to seeing his mom put out a nice spread every evening for dinner, so naturally he thought Angela should do the same thing. Except that Angela didn't get home from her office until around 6:00 p.m., and besides, the last thing she wanted to do after a long day of work was more work. She suggested a compromise: two days a week she would stop and get takeout, and the other two days they would go out to eat. And maybe the fifth day they could prepare a meal together. Tom resisted, saying that would cost too much, and that's when things really hit the fan.

"Look, with the kind of money we're making, I think we can afford takeout and Applebee's," Angela responded with more than a little sarcasm in her voice.

"But I've been making double payments each month on our mortgage so we can pay it off sooner," Tom responded.

"What?" Angela asked, her voice rising. "You never told me you were doing that."

"You never asked."

Then there was her first business trip. Angela's boss wanted her to accompany him on a trip to New York to try and land a new client. She was careful to let Tom know a few weeks in advance, but immediately sensed resistance.

"You're okay with this, aren't you?" she asked.

"I guess," he began. "But to be truthful, it makes me a little nervous."

"Nervous? How so?"

"Oh come on, Angela. You're an attractive woman. Your boss is divorced. You're going on a business trip to New York where you'll most likely have dinner with him."

"Oh, so you don't trust me ..."

"Of course I do, it's just ... things happen."

"So ..." She paused and then continued. "I should be worried when *you* travel, which is a lot more than I do, by the way."

"Well, that's different," he answered a bit defensively.

"Oh, so it's different because you're a guy and I'm a girl, huh?"

Even though this is a fictitious story, it parallels many I frequently hear from young professional women who are married. What should be a blessing to be enjoyed and celebrated—two great jobs with substantial incomes—becomes a wedge that gradually pushes them apart. From my own experience and observations, two factors contribute to making dual-income marriages so difficult. First, despite the time we live in, a lot of guys still struggle with the *effects* of their wives' careers. Or to put it another way, they have no problem with their wives working, until it creates a problem. Tom supported Angela's career as a lawyer until it required her to travel with her boss. The fact that Angela never interfered with *his* travel did not occur to him as a double standard. He expected her to trust him but did not reciprocate. He also didn't realize that his response to her upcoming trip was insulting. It suggested that he felt she was incapable of handling herself professionally, or too weak or vulnerable to refuse her boss's advances, should something like that even happen. The key to making a relationship work in this situation is for both people to come to a level of trust through faith in God and in each other.

I love it when Chris expresses concern for my safety when I travel, but there's a big difference between "Have a safe trip" and "I'm not sure you should travel because, you know, you're a woman and there will be a lot of men with you." One is an honest expression of love (that should go both ways), while the other is an attempt to control someone. (Chris never actually plays the control game or I probably wouldn't have married him. Not a big fan of control freaks.)

But an even bigger factor contributing to the challenges of dual-income marriages is actually part of the solution to the first one: communication. Tom's efforts to pay off the mortgage by doubling their monthly mortgage payments were a good thing that turned bad because he never discussed it with Angela. His concern for his wife on a business trip also was a good thing, but had they talked about business travel early in their marriage, he might not have come off sounding so distrustful and paternalistic. Communication contributes to the success of any marriage, but becomes even more critical in dual-career marriages because now there are two incomes to manage wisely, two work schedules to coordinate, and less time to do both.

When Chris and I got married, we each had our own balance sheets from our savings and checking accounts, our own separate investments, our own charities we supported, and our own work schedules that included a fair amount of travel, and our own kids' activities. Thankfully, we sat down even before we got married to first establish a "full disclosure" honesty policy regarding our incomes, expenses, work and family schedules, and we determined how we would make decisions regarding them. (See "The Couple that Plans Together" sidebar on page 173)

Regarding financial decisions, not a penny comes in that we both don't know about, nor does any bill get paid without each other's full knowledge. When our statements arrive, we look at our expenses versus our income on a monthly basis, plus, we discuss our balance sheet on a semiannual basis, including our charitable giving. When a major event occurs, such as a job change, we revisit all three. We have given each other permission to question anything. Fortunately, we're both pretty frugal, so there's seldom a need to question each other's expenses. But occasionally, a charge will show up that's significantly higher than normal and I might say something like, "What was that $2,300 charge for?" Instead of getting defensive or vague, he'll remind me that we replaced his laptop — something we both agreed was necessary, but it just slipped my mind.

The key to keeping these discussions from getting contentious is to remember who you're talking to. Chris is my husband, lover, and best friend, so if I have a question about our finances, why would I ask it like I am an IRS agent trying to catch a tax dodger? I think one reason so many couples argue over money is that they turn these discussions into an inquisition. The tone of your voice, your body language, the expression on your face can signal either animosity or partnership. If you cultivate a climate of trust in your marriage, you can actually enjoy your money talks rather than dread going over this month's bills. Confession: I have not always done this perfectly. I hate surprises, and Chris is not as verbal as I am, so sometimes he may have felt like he was being interrogated. But he's also very forgiving. Right, honey?

Separate or Joint?

In addition to establishing an open full-disclosure policy when it comes to finances, dual-income couples need to make decisions regarding their various accounts. Each couple is different, so I can't recommend which will work best for you, but here are some ways dual-career marriages do it:

Separate but open. My paycheck goes into my bank accounts; your paycheck goes into yours. And we both have access to each other's accounts. The advantage here is that it's relatively clean and simple and allows both of you to keep track of your income. The disadvantage is that it can cultivate a me/mine rather than an "ours" mentality. It also can create tension over who pays which bills. Do I use *my* checking account to pay for the groceries that everyone in the family eats and you pay only for those things that are yours?

One big pot. Basically, joint checking and savings accounts. In this scenario, you both agree on an amount to put in your savings account from each paycheck, and the rest goes into a joint checking account. This is the system we use. We have two checking accounts, one for the usual bills and one to save so we can cover the large-ticket items such as the taxes on our house, etc. All usual bills are paid from that joint checking account, usually with one person handling those responsibilities, and in our case it's Chris.

One checking, two savings. Each contributes an agreed-upon amount into a joint checking account which is used to pay bills. The rest from each paycheck goes into separate savings accounts for the person to do with as he or she pleases. This tends to preserve a sense of financial freedom for each while at the same time jointly contributing to regular expenses. The downside is that it often defeats the purpose of saving because it's too easy to use your savings account to spend unwisely.

Cash for fun. Many dual-income marriages suffer because one person spends too much. One way to prevent that is to agree on a specific amount of cash each person withholds from his or her paycheck. That's their money. If she wants to save each week until she has enough to buy a new set of golf clubs, no one can say, "Hey, we can't afford that right now." If he wants to spend his entire allowance each week on building his music collection, keep your mouth shut and enjoy the music.

Joint bank accounts, separate credit cards. Credit cards can be dangerous, especially if you're just starting out and your income doesn't quite cover your tastes. (The average credit-card debt per household with credit-card debt: $15,788.) On the other hand, monthly credit-card statements give both of you a crystal-clear look at your expenses. Separate credit cards make sense, but only if you follow the full-disclosure rule and go over your accounts together each month *and* are willing to make adjustments if you're spending too much. We have separate credit cards, plus separate ones for personal and business expenses.

More important than *how* you set up your various accounts is that you make these decisions together and that everything financial is an open book. I'm also a big fan of getting expert advice before making important financial decisions, and you can do this formally (professional financial advisor), or informally (trusted friends in similar situations, parent or relative, older colleague in a two-income marriage). Once you have all the information in front of you, go over it with your spouse and find a solution that fits your needs and that both of you support.

Fortunately, I was introduced to Erin Botsford and her Botsford Financial Group last year. I had just spent some time looking over our finances recently and realized God had protected us from a lawsuit because many of our assets weren't protected. In addition, I could have done a better job with our investments if I would have taken time earlier to think about the fact that God gave us the gifts that produced treasure for the kingdom. We could have planned our giving better earlier if we would have engaged a good financial planner that understood our eternal goals. Don't be afraid to seek professional help with your finances. (See Matthew 19:16–30 and www.moneyhelpforchristians .com/70-new-testament-bible-verses-about-money/.)

Men's Work, Women's Work

In addition to making decisions about how we handled our two incomes, we also spent time early in our marriage deciding who was going to do what when it came to household chores and other responsibilities. I can't tell you how to divide those things up with *your* husband, but our decisions were usually based on what each of us were good at and liked to do, so in terms of handling our finances, Chris does the day-to-day accounting while I manage our investments. Then there are those things that neither of us enjoys doing that much, so we try to divide those equally between us. Finally, there are those horrible things we both hate to do like clean the bathrooms or wash the windows, and that's when we realized what a blessing it was to have the income to afford a housekeeper. In addition, as our kids were growing up we gave them chores to do, often rotating them so that no one got stuck with the same chore.

The best advice I can give you regarding dividing up household chores with your spouse is to aim for fairness. Some men — and women, believe it or not — make the mistake of thinking women are better suited for things like the laundry, kitchen work, or housecleaning. If they really are *better* at those things it's usually because they've never had any choice in the matter. When it comes to housework, I am definitely pro-choice! Start with a clean slate and no assumptions about men's work or women's work. Chris does the laundry. I'm in charge of house management, such as organizing, making shopping lists, managing anyone who helps us, and so on. I know women who are so much better at keeping their vehicles maintained than most men, and I know men who love to cook *and* clean up after themselves (no kidding!). Actually, both Chris and I are decent cooks, so we share this responsibility along with sticking around to clean up. Dual-career families function best as a team, with everyone doing their fair share of the work.

When Mary Earns More than Harry

I'm not one to read *People* magazine regularly or to try and stay current on Hollywood gossip, but you'd have to be living on another planet not to know how difficult it is for the husbands of famous—and highly paid—actresses. Not naming any names here, but when a woman who commands millions for each film she makes is married to a guy who's never seen a six-figure salary, it isn't long before we read about their impending divorce. Whether or not you find those stories entertaining or intriguing or real, you might want to pay attention, because it could happen to you. Now more than ever before, more and more women are earning more money than their husbands. According to the Bureau of Labor Statistics, in 1987 17.8 percent of working wives whose husbands also worked earned more than their husbands. In 2006, that proportion grew to 25.7 percent.[6] With more women going to college now than men, experts say this trend will continue, so there's a pretty good chance you may bring home a bigger paycheck than your husband—if you aren't already.

You wouldn't think coming home with the news that your raise put you in a bracket higher than your husband would be a problem, but for many men it is. Part of the problem is that the majority of guys today grew up in homes where Dad brought home the bacon and if Mom worked at all, she contributed a lot less money to the family funds. They're just programmed into thinking they have to be just like Dad, so when you earn more than he does he struggles with a range of emotions: Does she think less of me now? Do I think less of myself? Will I have less of a say in our financial decisions?

Guys tend to be big on respect, and unfortunately in our society we place a high premium on how much money people make. So when the wife makes more than the husband, the husband senses that he's lost some respect. Guys also tend to be pretty competitive, and even though they may not consciously compete when it comes to his wife's income, when he learns that she's making more than him, he often feels as if he's coming in second when he's been used to being in the lead, even though

God doesn't view it that way. Finally, even in the most egalitarian marriages, men tend to view themselves as the provider, according to Scott Haltzman, author of *The Secrets of Happily Married Men*. "So when the man is generating less money, he feels personally responsible for his family's situation, and can feel that he is not doing enough to provide for his wife's happiness and the stability of his family," Haltzman says.[7]

If you find yourself in a position where you're earning significantly more money than your husband or boyfriend, you would be wise to take some advice from my good friend Lisbeth McNabb. Lisbeth is one of those people big companies call on to come in and take their company to the next level. About every five years—for the past twenty-five years— she joins a company, creates a blueprint for them to grow at a higher rate, executes the plan, and then builds a team to sustain the growth before leaving. A true innovator with entrepreneurial skills, she's paid extremely well for what she does. Several years ago she began dating a guy and it wasn't long before she sensed this was someone special with whom she could easily spend the rest of her life. Fortunately, he felt the same way.

"One day David said to me, 'We need to talk. I want you to know exactly who I am.' I wasn't sure what was coming next, but then he proceeded to pull out his W-2s and bank statements and shared with me details about his annual salary and financial assets. I really wasn't expecting that, but it was so characteristic of him, because I had come to know him as being very direct and honest."

In retrospect, Lisbeth realizes that even though she had never talked about her income, David suspected that she probably made a lot more money than he did and wanted to make sure she was comfortable marrying a journalist (at the time, a sportswriter for the *Dallas Morning News*) who would probably never see six figures.

"What attracted me to David was his passion for life and that he was more interested in doing work that he loved than making a lot of money," Lisbeth explained to me. "His values were more around a passion for his work rather than a passion for money."

Lisbeth recommends that as couples become serious and think about marriage, they need to have an honest conversation about money—especially if the woman has a job that pays well.

"It was so important that we had that conversation *before* we got married so that we both knew what we were getting into. I think one of the reasons David is so secure in our relationship is that he knows I respect him for who he is and the great work he does as a journalist. If we hadn't addressed it directly, the disparity in our incomes might have become a barrier to our relationship."

As Christians, both David and Lisbeth feel the church sometimes contributes to guys feeling inferior if they aren't the chief breadwinner.

"For us, it's an issue of stewardship. I've been given certain skills that allow me to earn a lot of money which also allows us to generously support God's work. From a biblical perspective, it wouldn't make sense for me to quit my job or deliberately try to earn less than David just so he can be saying he's bringing home more money than I [do]."

With more women earning advanced degrees than ever before and now outnumbering men in the workplace, the traditional "dad goes to work, mom stays home" couple will become obsolete, if it already hasn't. And the chances that you will earn more than your boyfriend or husband are only going to increase. The key to success in any relationship is communication, and if you're both involved in challenging careers, the need to slow down and make sure you're on the same page is even greater. Chris and I couldn't survive if we didn't deliberately set aside time to coordinate our schedules, review our finances, and share both our joys and our concerns.

Knowing you have a teammate at home makes it a lot easier to deal with some of the loneliness you are sure to feel as a woman in the workplace.

For Reflection and Discussion

1. In what ways is your experience as a woman different from your mother's? Your grandmother's?

2. Most experts point to money as one of the primary sources of friction in a marriage. Why do you think money causes so many arguments in marriage? How are you going to communicate openly and lovingly with each other about financial matters?

3. In what ways does popular culture (media, movies, etc.) reinforce the idea that your value as a person is closely tied to how much money you make? Give examples. What can you do to reinforce with your spouse or boyfriend that the amount of money you make is not the key ingredient to a strong relationship?

4. If you are married and both you and your husband are working, how do you handle your money? Who makes decisions about major purchases? How do you resolve disputes about money?

5. How do you and your husband deal with travel? How do you coordinate schedules so that one is not feeling the burden of the responsibilities at home?

6. How satisfied are you with the way your husband deals with money issues? What could you both do to improve? How do you communicate around your schedules so that you make sure that each other is aware of the week ahead without hidden surprises?

God's Minimum Standards of Finance

God owns everything. *"We have brought nothing into the world, so we cannot take anything out of it either"* (1 Timothy 6:7 NASB). Once couples accept the fact that God owns everything and that they have been chosen to be stewards or managers of God's property, it's important for them to manage according to his principles and standards. Since in a marriage a husband and wife are one, the financial assets and incomes of both husband and wife should be merged and they should operate from a unified financial-management base rather than from a separate and independent management base.

Think ahead and avoid problems. *"Which one of you, when he wants to build a tower, does not first sit down and calculate the cost to see if he has enough to complete it?"* (Luke 14:28 NASB). Too often couples put off planning until they are so deeply in debt or into the marriage that it seems impossible to get out. By then it is too late to plan, except for crisis planning. Couples need to begin planning by writing down their goals and objectives, which should include a yearly balanced budget.

Keep good records. *"By wisdom a house is built, and by understanding it is established; and by knowledge the rooms are filled with all precious and pleasant riches"* (Proverbs 24:3–4 NASB). Recently it was discovered that fewer than two out of ten couples know how to actually balance their checkbooks. This means that many married couples seldom know how much money they have to spend or how much they are spending. Couples should develop their financial plans together and work together, but there should be only one bookkeeper in the home who pays the bills. Two bookkeepers invites bookkeeping disaster.

Get educated. *"The naive believes everything, but the sensible man considers his steps"* (Proverbs 14:15 NASB). Most financially naive couples are not stupid regarding money; they are just ignorant and do not understand how borrowing and interest rates work. As a result, their primary concern becomes, "How much are the monthly payments?" rather than "How much is this going to cost ultimately?" Couples need to learn financial management and budgeting and use that information to avoid debt or financial problems.[8]

The Couple that Plans Together

With two careers, a wonderfully blended family, and our own individual interests, things can get pretty hectic for us. So once each year, Chris and I carve out some time to set our goals for the various areas of our lives. Here's the outline we follow:

I. Each of us individually set goals for these areas:
  A. Spiritual
    1. Bible study
    2. Accountability group
    3. Worship
    4. Prayer time
    5. Seminars, retreats, etc.
  B. Physical
    1. Exercise
    2. Healthy eating

    C. Family and friends
       1. My husband, Chris, and things we need to work on
       2. My children, Annie and Opie, and my focus on
          them
       3. Our blended family—all six of us—and what I can
          contribute to each of them
       4. My extended family—plans to visit and needs they
          might have that I can address
       5. My friends–what I need to do to maintain close
          personal relationships
    D. Professional
       1. My career plans
       2. My not-for-profit ministry (4word)
    E. Community—where I will volunteer and/or donate

II. Then, Chris and I sit down and talk about our respective goals for the dimensions of our lives listed above. We compare notes to make sure we're on the same page, make adjustments where necessary, and learn as much as we can from each other.

III. Finally, we go over the following areas together:
    A. Financial goals and planning
       1. Income, expenses, giving, and saving
       2. Investments and other money matters
    B. Housing—Any needs related to our primary residence, other properties, and mortgages

Not only does this process help us manage our busy lives, but it also deepens our relationship by examining what's important to each other.

a little help
from your friends

IF YOU HAVEN'T ALREADY DISCOVERED THIS, here's how things really get done in the business world:

You're in a meeting, dealing with the same old budget issues. The CEO chairs the meeting, and your boss, a vice president, is presenting the numbers from your division which has done pretty well this quarter. You're feeling a little smug because you found a way to trim expenses by about 20 percent, which contributed to the good numbers and looks of envy from the other divisions nervously waiting to report. Overall, only two of the four divisions beat their budgets, and your division came out on top for the quarter. As he adjourned the meeting, the CEO looked over the table to the three other VPs and said, "Hey, I need one of you to help me complete a foursome at the club tonight. Anyone up for it?"

Now you would think the CEO might have asked your boss to join him. Golfing with the CEO might have been a nice little reward for your division's performance for the quarter. Four hours to bend his ear, talk a little shop, maybe run some initiatives by him that will need his support if they have even the slightest chance of getting launched. Even though it was your boss who actually got overlooked, you feel a little slighted too because of all the hard work you put in that helped your division shine. The CEO's a great guy and an excellent leader, so why would he ask one of the other VPs to spend four hours with him on the golf course?

Because your boss is a woman.

Women don't get invited to play golf with the boss. Men do. Women don't get asked to have drinks with the guys on Friday afternoon. When the boss wants to kibitz with someone in the middle of the morning, you don't see him joking and laughing with a group of women. And obviously, women can't enter that sacred place where, truth be told, a lot of business gets done: The Men's Room. (Of course, I am generalizing, because there are more women VPs today than thirty years ago, but the number of women CEOs of Fortune 500 companies is at fifteen.)

I'm not saying we even *want* to sit around and joke with the boss or have a drink with him after hours, but the fact that we seldom get invited into the inner circle underscores a sad reality about the marketplace: despite all the progress women have made, it's still pretty much a good ol' boys network out here. Over the years I've observed women respond to this reality in one of two ways. In most cases, women just complain among themselves about it. Occasionally, I'll see a woman trying to insert herself into that men's club. Complaining never accomplishes anything and is a big time waster. And if women only knew how unprofessional it looks for them to try to gain entry without invitation into the network, they would quit trying.

Frankly, sometimes we women are our own worst enemies in the workplace, and in the case of the male-dominated business environment, here's a startling fact to ponder: you're not a man. That doesn't mean you should tolerate anything but equal and fair treatment, but you're not going to help yourself by complaining or bugging the guys for an invitation to their Thursday night card game.

Which reminds me of a young professional I'll call Melissa. Melissa worked for a large advertising agency in the Midwest. She was ambitious, smart, and energetic and almost immediately caught the attention of her boss who promoted her within six months. Somewhat idealistic, when Melissa discovered the good ol' boys network, she made it her mission to join. If she overheard one of the guys talking to another guy about getting together for drinks after work, she asked if she could join. During breaks in meetings when she saw her boss in the corner with a couple of guys laughing, she made it a point to wander over in their direction and just sort of listen in. Her boss, a friend of mine, wasn't sure what to make of it.

"I probably shouldn't feel this way, but this very nice young woman who everyone liked became something of a pest," he said. "Do I tend to hang out with the guys? Yes, and maybe I could do a better job of inviting Melissa and other women to join us. But old habits die hard, I guess. It just seems as if she went about it all wrong."

I'm not sure I totally buy my friend's explanation, but I decided to give him a pass because he raised an issue that resonates with my own thinking: there's a right way and a wrong way for everything. Regardless of the business or enterprise, relationships are important and often necessary for your growth within the company. Do men tend to form their closest relationships with each other? Absolutely. Is that necessarily a barrier to women? Absolutely not! I've never let the fact that men like to hang out with each other stand in my way, and neither should you. There's no reason for you to feel isolated as a woman in a male-dominated environment, just as there's no reason you can't develop rewarding relationships with men. Maybe there are other women feeling the same way who will become good friends to help you through this environment. It's all about how you go about it.

Strength in Numbers

You would think that with so many of us in the workplace — now more women than men — we wouldn't feel so isolated. But a lot of women do — sometimes it's almost as if we're on an island in the middle of the ocean. This might seem like a simple thing, but the go-out-to-lunch groups usually don't include women. Who's usually eating alone? Usually, more women than men. The guys seem to have their little clubs that hold "official" meetings during lunch or on breaks, but we keep our noses to the grindstone and pretty much go it alone. What's with *that*?

Part of the reason women often feel isolated at work is because we don't have the luxury to stick around after hours for some of the activities the guys enjoy because we have kids to care for. For women with children—especially single moms—their lives are pretty regimented: get up and get the kids ready, drop them off at day care on the way to work, put in your eight hours and rush to pick up the kids on time and then home. Even when we have some help with the kids, we're usually too tired to meet up after work—assuming we're even invited.

But what's stopping you from forming your own relationships with other *women*, on your terms and suited to your timetable? Just because the boys won't let you play on their team doesn't mean you have to be a loner. Maybe it's because I had such a great experience in my college sorority and college activities, but I've always found ways to connect with other professional women, which is why I've never really felt isolated or alone.

One of the best ways to build helpful networks of other professional women is to join a professional association related to your particular career or area of expertise. Most of these associations sponsor national, regional, even local events where you not only keep up with the latest developments in your field, but have opportunities to meet and form relationships with other women. In my own field of commercial real estate, I've belonged to two trade associations, and when I attend their national conventions, they always sponsor a women's reception sometime during the event. These "women only" events have given me dozens of strategic friendships that have lasted throughout my career. In fact, just recently I received an email out of the blue from a woman I met several years ago at a conference sponsored by Commercial Real Estate Women (CREW).

She thought that since we were both now senior-level executives in major firms with our children approaching adulthood, it would be good to reconnect and compare notes about this particular stage in our careers.

My one caution here is to avoid getting so involved in the association that it takes over all your free time—and it can happen because they depend so much on volunteers to help them run the organization. Focus on what benefits you most and especially take advantage of the opportunities they provide to build relationships with other professional women. Early in life before children or if you don't have children or later in life when your kids have grown may be better times to get more involved with these organizations. I recently have gotten much more involved with CREW. Previously, my faith, family, and career, which included travel, was enough to consume my time. Now, my children are grown and at college, so travel is not an issue like it was before. Kids need your time to feel important and your work alone will provide competition.

In addition to professional associations dedicated to your specific career, you might also consider professional organizations targeted exclusively to women (see appendix in the back of this book). For example, the National Association of Professional Women (www.napw.com) provides national training seminars, mentorship programs, and local chapters, along with a directory that includes personal profiles to help you locate other members in your area who are in a similar career. Their mission says it all: to provide the most advanced and exclusive forum for members to find like-minded professional women to create innovative business and social relationships, while delivering a wealth of resources and benefits to foster professional and personal success.

You might also consider joining one of the several excellent professional associations that offer a Christian perspective. The National Association of Christian Women in Business (www.nacwib.com) is largely a web-based association that focuses primarily on entrepreneurs and business owners. It's free, provides online training, and helps connect Christian women in the business community.

While not exclusive to women, Campus Crusade for Christ has launched an impressive association, Priority Associates (www.priorityassociates.org), targeted to young men and women in the business community who are "making decisions that will affect them for the rest of their lives." Its primary focus is to help you live the way God wants us to in the workplace, and it provides resources to help you do that. With local chapters in twenty-four major U.S. cities (and growing), it also sponsors outreach opportunities for its members.

In addition to connecting with other professional women through these formal associations, you can just as easily informally develop relationships with women in your company. All it takes is some initiative to form your own "good ol' girls network." Sort of "if you can't join 'em, beat 'em" approach to the boys' club in your office. Chances are, all those other young professional women you occasionally run into in your office are feeling the same way and are waiting for someone to break the ice. The richness I enjoyed while at Trammell Crow Company and CB Richard Ellis grew out of my relationships with Linda, Theresa, Susan, Lisa, Kate, Karen, Melissa, Jesse, and many more.

Remember Melissa, the young woman who kept trying to break into the boys' club? She would have benefited more from using her outgoing personality to develop relationships with other women before she tried to hang out with the guys. There are ways to network with men in your company which we'll look at later, but to find the support you're looking for, connect first with a few women who face the same challenges you do and who can be there for you as you negotiate your way through everything from office politics to not having to eat lunch alone. In Hebrews 10:25 we are told to encourage one another. So being in fellowship with other believers at work will be a real support to you.

Here's a quick little tip for finding other women like you. If you achieve frequent-flier status and get upgraded to business or first class on a flight, the other women in that section of the plane are most likely a lot like you. They're traveling because of their job. They are surrounded by men all day. And whether married or single, they don't have too many friends who understand what their lives are like. One of the closest friends I have today, Nancy Alsgard, I met on such a flight. We struck up a conversation and have stayed close ever since. Had I buried my face in a book or put on my "don't bother me" face, I would have missed out on discovering one of my greatest allies in this adventure of balancing faith, family, and work. I have not only made women friends, but professional men friends from conversations on airplanes.

Finally, pay attention when you meet other young women in your city. When I first moved to Dallas, I met a delightful young woman who had a position in an oil business. I learned that she was a Christian, had small children, and was divorced. After graduate school, good friends of mine from Harvard Business School, Vaughn Brock, Joel Manby, Dougal Cameron, and Kevin Jenkins formed a small group of men united in the name of Jesus Christ by their faith and their professional careers. They stay in touch and get together as often as possible, sort of like an accountability group. Their families are close too. It's been twenty-five years. I've always longed for what they had so I decided to just step up to the plate and ask my friend Savannah if she'd like to join me in forming a similar small group.

"I'd love to!" she answered.

Shortly after, I met a woman through my own company, Sue, who had come to faith as an adult. When I invited her into our new little group, she too readily agreed. In no time, we were joined by a woman who ran her own company, Brenda Buell, a person I admired due to our relationship in a ranch in which we were both partners, and Claire Horn, a physician. Each joined us in the pursuit of God while still working and fulfilling the roles God has gifted us to do. We began meeting every other week just to talk about our lives, our careers, our families, and our faith. The key to our success is that we keep it informal and there are no rules. If you can't make one of our get-togethers, no one complains; there are no guilt trips to deal with. In fact, we began by agreeing that this informal group meeting would be a bonus, not a burden. Though we represented different types of businesses, we all have similar challenges: marriage, having been divorced, managing the demands of being a "good mom" while working, managing people, working in male-dominated workplaces, and dealing with pretty high expectations to perform well (either imposed by others or ourselves).

Almost from the beginning, it became clear that no topic was off-limits. We shared things with each other about our marriages that we might not have felt like we could share even with a marriage counselor. One time one of the women in our group sold her business then bought it back after the buyers were not what she expected, and she shared details about the situation that could never have been made public. And another time, one in our group opened up about how she felt she had lost her excitement and passion for God. Teenagers acting out. Kids with learning disabilities. Divorce. This is no knitting club where we share recipes and joke about our husbands. And nothing against Bible studies, but this isn't a Bible study, although we spend a lot of time praying for each other. We get down and dirty, but the support we all get from each other is amazing. We just took a break after eighteen months and I really miss them.

When you have "sisters" like that, who needs to join the boys' club?

These all-girl relationships—whether within your company or crossing over into other industries—help resolve that "alone on an island" feeling you can easily get as a young professional Christian woman. There *are* a lot more people like you out there than you think. All it takes is a little initiative on your part to find a few kindred spirits to confide in and draw strength from. But there's yet another type of relationship for you to consider, and it will include both men and women. I call them "strategic friendships" because they can be critical to your ongoing success in your company. It is wonderful if these strategic relationships are with believers, so that your advice comes from someone who is seeking what God wants in your life first; but if friendship with a believer isn't possible, then seek out someone whom you know lives by strong ethical and moral standards.

Connecting with People of Influence

You've probably already learned this cardinal rule of the workplace: who you know is almost as important as what you know. Or, to give that a more positive spin, I like to borrow from the old Beatles song — we all benefit from "a little help from our friends." I'm not talking about sucking up or trying to get anything you don't deserve. You can be best friends with the CEO, but if you don't have what it takes to get the job done well, you're not going to be successful. On the other hand, it just makes sense to develop allies within and without your company or organization who can help you negotiate the office politics and other intricacies that can either help or hinder your growth. However, a word of caution. Don't force a relationship that doesn't naturally jell. It won't work or feel authentic to them either.

When I first got to Trammell Crow, there were two people in senior positions who seemed to take an interest in me. If you haven't already, you will experience the same thing, for great leaders are all about developing talent within the company. These are the kinds of people you need to pay attention to, not to score points or in some way try to exploit their friendship for your gain, but to learn from and consult with whenever you aren't quite sure what to do next.

As you discover those people in your company who seem to be as interested in your success as you are, be up-front and honest with them about your career. When Don Williams, the chairman at the time at Trammell Crow, would stop by my office and offer a word of encouragement or ask me how I was doing when we ran into each other, it opened the door for us to get to know each other better, and that's when I learned that God and his family were the priorities in his life. So I swallowed hard one day and mustered up all my courage and asked him if I could go to him from time to time for advice — to have him serve as a mentor to me, and he graciously and enthusiastically agreed. Also, remember to do the same thing for others, as God also asks us to help those who are coming behind us (Romans 12:16).

Maintain Healthy Boundaries

In every healthy company there are people in leadership who look for the "rising stars" and find ways to help them grow. And yes, a lot of these influential people in your company will be men, and here's where it can get a little dicey.

A woman I'll call Carrie was a young, successful sales rep for a major pharmaceutical company. Her star was rising fast, and she spent about four days a week on the road with her regional sales manager and his technical adviser. Both were men, and both liked to end a long day in the hotel lounge enjoying a few drinks.

"I knew that my regional manager held the key to my future in the company and that joining him and his buddy in the lounge would be a good thing careerwise," she recounted. "But it didn't feel comfortable to me, and it certainly didn't sit well with my husband."

Now I don't want to suggest that every guy who invites you to join him for a drink after work is trying to hit on you. In fact, it's been my experience that most guys—especially in senior leadership—are principled men who have treated me with respect and would never interfere with my career if I didn't hang out with them after hours. On the other hand, we're all human, and if you keep even a cursory eye on the news, you know that hardly a week goes by without some salacious story about a boss having an affair with a younger employee. How do you nurture healthy, strategic relationships with men in your company without communicating the wrong message or putting yourself in an awkward situation?

This may sound idealistic and even a little trite, but your faith is the first place to start when it comes to keeping these relationships professional. Staying close to God's Word, regularly worshipping with other believers, participating in a small group of other Christian women you can open up to completely and who will hold you accountable as well as hold you up in prayer—these are the kinds of things that will help you keep your priorities straight. But I also believe that our faith needs to translate into action, and in this case that means applying some common-sense, practical advice to our interactions with men in the workplace.

Always be in control. If you're pounding shots with the guys in the hotel bar, your good judgment is going to fade with every drink. And if someone's encouraging you to try and "keep up with the guys," he's not your friend. Similarly, if you order a soda and anyone gives you grief, it might be a good time to find another person to talk with. It's never a good idea to have too much to drink; adding men and a road trip increases the odds of something happening that you'll later regret (Ephesians 5:18).

Be one of the first to leave. These late-night soirees usually begin with a large group and then dwindle as people call it a night. I'll often join my colleagues at these gatherings because it helps build team spirit and to be honest, I enjoy the camaraderie. But when the first person gets up to leave, that's my cue to bid everyone a good night and head back to my room. I'm typically in my room by 10:00 p.m.

Dress appropriately. You communicate a lot by how you dress. After a long day of running through airports, sitting through meetings, and negotiating deals, it's perfectly normal to want to slip into something comfortable and kick back with your colleagues. Comfortable is fine as long as it isn't too revealing or suggestive. The men I respect in business tell me that women who put their stuff out there for everyone to see are a joke and are never taken seriously. Sometimes a guy will even ask me to speak to women who tend to wear tight or revealing clothing (Mark 9:42).

Keep your boundaries in place. If you're married or have children, find a way to work them into your conversation. It's a subtle way to say "I'm not interested" to anyone who might be looking. If you're single and one of the guys seems headed where you're not interested in going, a couple of pleasantly delivered lines will turn him into a perfect gentleman: "How well do you know Jim, our VP of human resources?"

Keep your hands to yourself. A lot of us women are very animated when we talk, and it's not unusual when I'm with my friends to place a hand on someone's shoulder or reach out and touch someone's arm as I'm talking to him. Not a good idea to do that on the job or after hours with men. Guys will read way more into that than you intend.

Listen to office gossip. Okay, normally I'm not a fan of gossip, but over time you learn a lot about people by listening to water-cooler conversations and Monday-morning accounts of the weekend's exploits. In other words, if you pay attention, you'll soon learn who the "players" are. You know what I'm talking about. The guys who have a reputation for flirting or partying hard. If you find yourself on the road with someone like that, keep your distance. Gossip isn't always accurate, but reputations are earned, and it doesn't take long to discover who the jerks are. Remember, Jesus doesn't want us to judge, but we also must be smart with information we receive.

Be professional after hours. Whether you're joining colleagues for dinner after work or traveling on your company's dime, keep your relationships on the professional level. If the conversation heads toward personal matters, steer it back on course. Most improper relationships begin with people sharing details about their personal lives.

Like I said, I've found "men behaving badly" to be the exception in the business world. To be fair, women haven't always had a stellar reputation in this department either. That should never stand in your way of developing strategic friendships to help you grow in your career. Few people achieve success completely on their own, and I owe it all to God. He provided me with women *and* men who have taken an interest in me and helped me achieve my dreams. I'm not sure what it's like at your company, but I'd be willing to bet there are at least a handful of people in senior management who would love to help you grow. And I'm absolutely certain there are women within your circle of influence who would accept your invitation to meet regularly to support each other as professional Christian women.

Both types of friendships will not only support your efforts to grow and become successful; they'll also be there for you when things don't go exactly according to plan. And trust me: life will throw you some devastating curveballs.

For Reflection and Discussion

1. In what ways have you felt isolated or "left out" at work? What can you do to change that situation?
2. Do you agree with the author that despite gains made by women in the marketplace it's still a man's world at work? Why or why not?
3. What has been your experience in trying to develop relationships with other women at work? Whom can you trust, support, and receive support from or have fun with?
4. Identify four to five women you would enjoy meeting with on a regular basis just to share your lives. What, if anything, is preventing you from starting such a group?
5. Have you ever experienced unwanted attention from men you work with? How did you deal with it?
6. How do you walk the fine line between developing strategic friendships with men without sending the wrong messages or putting yourself in an awkward position? Who would be a natural, easy, beneficial, and professional person to go to and ask them to be your mentor?

Start Your Own Group of Professional Women Friends

One of the best things I ever did for myself was to recruit a few women to join me every two weeks to talk about our lives over lunch. You can do it too. Just follow these simple directions:

1. **Keep it simple.** No agenda. No book to study. No pressure to maintain perfect attendance. And don't meet too often. Our group meets every other week over lunch. We figured, "Everyone has to eat lunch, so let's combine a meal with some good, heart-to-heart conversation."

2. **Keep it relational.** This isn't a Bible study. It's about "us." Our lives. The things that keep us up at night. And we don't try to solve each other's problems. Just listen, care, and pray.

3. **Keep it small.** Too many people require longer meetings and almost insure you never get beyond superficial conversation. Five or less is best.

4. **Keep it fluid.** By that I mean, don't think of your group as being a permanent appointment on your calendar. If interest wanes or the group isn't meshing, give yourselves permission to stop. Or take a few months off. Most of us have way too many meetings to turn this into just another obligation.

5. **Keep it confidential.** Invite women with whom you've had some history and know you can trust. Figuratively, join hands and vow to each other, "What's said at this table stays at this table."

6. **Keep it within your generation.** You will have many similar issues around which to connect and support each other due to the stage of life you are experiencing at the time.

7. **Keep it out of your company.** For this type of group, it works best to draw from people outside your company. You won't get bogged down in office issues, and you'll be more likely to be completely honest with each other.

Navigating Relationships

When Linda Lindquist-Bishop goes to work, she's surrounded by men. Sometimes she even sleeps with them, but it's not what you think.

Lindquist-Bishop, who owns her own consulting firm and has held executive positions in a variety of businesses, is also a world-class sailor. She has two world championships under her belt and made history as a member of *America3*, the first all-women's team to compete in the legendary America's Cup. Her "office" is often a cramped, damp cabin bouncing around on twelve-foot waves.

When you're in the middle of the ocean trying to win a race and have a chance to grab a rare couple hours of sleep, you don't exactly have a private stateroom. You find whatever empty space you can and if that means you're within snoring distance of one of the ten guys on board, you just hope he doesn't hear you.

Whatever glamour is left quickly disappears when you see the bathroom: a plastic bucket.

Throughout her career in business and competitive racing, Lindquist-Bishop has developed close friendships with hundreds of men. How has she kept those friendships on the up-and-up?

"I know it may sound simplistic, but you just don't date guys in your work environment," she explains. "Once you veer down that path, you're heading for trouble, and I've seen it happen to so many women. Besides, I never wanted to be accused of sleeping my way to a promotion or opportunity."

Her sailing career has taken her all over the world and between the legendary parties and ruggedly handsome men, there's enough to make Brian, her husband, nervous. So how do they deal with her often weeks-long excursions?

"It's all about doing the things that build trust," Lindquist-Bishop explains. "Since day one of our dating, I made sure Brian knew everything I did when I was with a team. When possible he joins me at an event to meet and build relationships with the guys. I always copy him on any emails of a personal nature that go out to my teammates. You can't have trust in a relationship if you keep your work life secret from your husband."

It's a two-way street for the couple, as Brian is an air force general and fighter pilot who is often deployed for long periods of time in places like Iraq, Korea, and Saudi Arabia.

"Brian's a dynamic and attractive guy — he used to be the lead pilot for the Thunderbirds, the air force's ace precision flying team. Our relationship would never survive without complete trust in each other."

On the practical side, Lindquist-Bishop, who was awarded *Glamour* magazine's "Women of the Year" in 1995, recommends a few safeguards to help women maintain their integrity in the work environment.

"A lot of it is common sense. Don't hang out in bars by yourself. I enjoy a great glass of wine as much as anyone, but never underestimate the power of alcohol to cloud your (or someone else's) judgment. Also, nothing productive happens in the business environment after 10:00 p.m., so go back to your hotel room after dinner.

She also leans heavily on her trust in God.

"I pray every day for discernment in my relationships, and I also have some great Christian friends who I ask to pray for me and also to hold me accountable."

That doesn't mean it's easy being one of very few women in mostly male environments.

"A few years ago I almost gave up racing because the global jet-setting lifestyle and bad-boy culture really started to get to me," Lindquist-Bishop recounts. "But God helped me see that he was giving me opportunities to have quiet conversations with some of these men that allowed me to share my faith and hope. I started to realize that God had put me on *this* career path for a reason. Before I leave for a regatta I now have a group of people praying for me that God will give me openings for deep meaningful dialogue and the strength to follow through on his behalf."

Though she has moved thirty times since college, Lindquist-Bishop has always been active in church life and seeks out the experience of a faith community in whatever corner of the world she happens to find herself. Currently she co-leads a women's Bible study in her small-town Michigan church, and attends a dynamic diverse church with her husband in Washington, D.C.

"God shows up in all of it!"

no one's perfect

NANCY ALSGARD HAD IT ALL. She married her childhood sweetheart—a guy she had known since they were both in the fifth grade in her little country school in Michigan. Both enjoyed good jobs, and she was finding her stride balancing her work, her marriage, their two young children, and her faith. Then within a brief span of time one of her brothers was reported missing in action in Vietnam (to this day is still MIA), her mom became afflicted with multiple sclerosis, her dad left her mom for another woman, and her husband was killed in an auto accident.

Blessed with a strong faith in God and the belief that she could turn grief into opportunity, she realized she would have to earn more money than her nurse's salary to keep a roof over her head and food on the table. She launched the first hospital-based oncology home-care program that became quite successful, moved from Michigan to Texas, fell in love, and got remarried. Once again, things were looking great for Nancy until her teenagers began acting out. Behavior problems. Drugs. Nothing that many parents haven't experienced, but for Nancy, it felt like failure. To make matters worse, after she sold her company she signed on to help with another health-care company and suddenly found herself fighting the good ol' boys club.

"I was the first person hired in at my level who didn't come from a business-school background, and you could almost feel the resentment from my colleagues," Nancy recalls. "I learned later that it normally took someone more than ten years to get to the level I hired in at, which was probably why I took a lot of arrows in the back."

Initially, Nancy struggled with guilt over her kids' problems but came to a place where she could forgive herself. "I wasn't the best mom in the world. I wasn't flawless. I made mistakes. But mistakes are a part of life. If you own them and don't blame others, you'll find a way to get through them and become a better person because of it." In these situations, God wants you to hand every part of your life to him so that you are free from guilt.

I wish I could tell you that Nancy's story is an exception, but the truth is, I've heard variations of this story from dozens of women. The details may differ, but the theme is the same: "I tried hard to be the best at everything, but I made some huge mistakes along the way." My sense of pride wishes I could tell you that *my* story doesn't include any imperfections, but I have to be honest: I've made more than my share of mistakes as a follower of Jesus, a wife, mom, and employee.

For some reason, we women set pretty high standards for ourselves and then torture ourselves when we don't measure up. According to a study conducted by researchers at Auburn University, women are more likely to have perfectionist tendencies than men.[1] Part of it surely has to do with the fact that we not only want to prove that we can balance our work with our family responsibilities, but that we can do it well. None of us want to be average at work and slightly above average at home. We want to be the best at both. So when we slip up along the way — or experience a major setback — we bring out the F word: failure.

Even though I was never handed a silver spoon as a younger girl, my growing-up years were about as close to perfect as you could get. Close, loving family where we all worked together on the farm. Nurturing community and church. Rural school that gave me opportunities to excel in the classroom and in extracurricular activities. Then off to four years of a fabulous college experience, a good job, Harvard. What more could a girl ask for?

So when my first marriage failed, I thought it wasn't my *marriage* that failed. It was me! Regardless of where "blame" actually fell, I put it all on me. *I* was the one who messed up. *I* should have made a better choice. *I* should have prayed more about whom to marry. *I* should have worked harder on my marriage. Instead, I failed. I grew up believing that marriage was forever. My parents have been married for fifty-four years, and my grandparents were married for forty-four when my grandfather died. Divorce wasn't an option. I never really thought my life was perfect, but something like this was never supposed to happen. It wasn't in my carefully executed life plan; it was God's plan.

My divorce was really the first big upset I had experienced, and it hurt. It was literally gut wrenching. But there were other reminders along the way that told me I didn't always measure up. As much as I tried to be there for my kids when they needed me, I know what it's like to feel the guilt that comes from missing a soccer game that your child expected you to attend. My relationship with God has always been important to me; however, I still forget to get into the Word every day like I should. I also know that there have been times when I wasn't the encouraging leader I wanted to be, as I let the stress of my job and my own competitive nature dim my witness as a woman of faith in the marketplace.

In other words, I'm human. And you are too. Not every presentation you make is going to light up the room and garnish a big pat on the back from your boss. Even if you are living every moment like Christ, you're going to have one of those days where you're sure your colleagues think you learned your interpersonal relationship skills from Cruella Devil. There are going to be days when you have to accept that you're an okay mom, not the best. And a so-so wife.

The Superwoman Myth

I really do believe you can have it all: a relationship with the Creator-God, a supportive family, and a rewarding career, but there's a big difference between comfortably balancing the things that are important to you and trying to be superwoman. I'm sure you've seen her. And heard her. She always looks fabulous, her kids are all honor students *and* star athletes, her husband not only remembers their anniversary but sends flowers to her desk, and she leads a Bible study every Tuesday night for three hundred women! Meanwhile, you're lucky you haven't lost an eye from applying your makeup in the car, and you have to leave work in the middle of the day because one of your kids got in a fight ... in kindergarten! Your husband does his best, but he's a guy. Just go to a Hallmark store just before closing the night before Valentine's Day and you'll know what I mean. And the last formal Bible study you attended? Forget about it.

Maybe superwoman really does exist, but I doubt it. Like you, I've measured myself against some of those perfectly coiffed women who appear to live charmed lives, telling myself I need to try harder so I can be just like her. Until a woman I thought had it all together confided in me that she and her husband were separating. I was shocked, because everything in her life seemed so perfect. It reminded me that all of us try to put our best face forward, and that maybe some people looked at me and thought *I* was all that. It's kind of like people who go to casinos all the time. You always hear about it when they win, but when was the last time you heard someone say, "I went to the casino last night and lost five hundred dollars."

Truth be told, someone's probably looking at you right now and wishing she had your life because it seems so perfect. But we know better, right?

It doesn't help that just about every Mother's Day, the preacher chooses Proverbs 31 for his text. You know, the "Proverbs 31 Woman." This is one woman I want to meet. She gets up before sunrise every morning to make a big breakfast for her family before she goes out and buys more land for her vineyard that brings in a lot of money. She helps the poor. In addition to running the vineyard, she makes clothes and sells them, manages the household finances, and even shovels the snow in the winter. No wonder "her children arise and call her blessed" (v. 28). Don't you just love it when a man stands up in the pulpit and tells every woman in the congregation this is what God wants you to be? And nothing against the Good Book, but how is it that David sleeps with another man's wife then sends her husband to the front lines of a battle where he gets killed and he's considered special by God, but we have to bring our husbands "good, not harm" all the days of our lives (v. 12)?

Of course I'm only joking, but sometimes the church inadvertently and unintentionally teaches that women *and* men (David and Bathsheba notwithstanding) have to be perfect. Like I said, I don't think any pastor really tries to teach us that, but we hear all these wonderful sermons about what we *should* be doing to be more Christlike and enjoy the lives God intends for us that after a while we start to believe we have to wear smiley faces all the time. Otherwise, people will think we're not *real* Christians. If you're having problems in your marriage or your kids are acting out, it must mean you've wandered outside God's will. Or that there's sin in your life. Of course, we don't want anyone to think we aren't wonderful Christians, so we deal with this bad theology in one of two ways. Men *pretend* everything's fine, while women just work harder and harder to try and make everything fine. Both responses are ultimately destructive. The hypocrite struggles endlessly with guilt, while the person who tries harder eventually crashes because no matter how hard you work, we all make mistakes.

Coping Strategies

Most of the time, the things that cause us so much grief are really tiny, but we give them more power over us than they deserve. Once, early in my career, I worked with this guy who really wasn't suited for the job he had, and for some reason I let his incompetence get under my skin. It got to the point where all I could think of at work was what a lousy match he was for the position he had and why no one would do anything about it. In retrospect, he wasn't my problem, *I* was. I was wrong to focus so much of my time and energy on my frustrations, and it affected the way I did my own job.

I can't say I'm thankful for the mistakes I've made—who would be? But I'm grateful for the lessons they have taught me:

Failing at something doesn't make you a failure. Never define yourself by your failures. Women tend to do that because we so want to succeed. But if you forgot to give your child her lunch money, you're not a failure as a mom. You forgot to do something. Big deal. Your daughter didn't starve, you're not the only mother in the world who's done this, and this one mistake doesn't negate all the nights you were up with her when she was a baby, all the meals you've shared, all the times she's told you she loves you. You're a good mom who is a normal human being. When you make a mistake—whether it's at home or at work—get over it and move on with your head held high.

Accept the limitations of being human. No one can keep the plates spinning all the time without one dropping occasionally. Balancing three things as important and challenging as a career, marriage and family responsibilities, and your relationship with God is a big assignment. You're not going to score an A plus all the time in all three areas. More often than not, you're going to pull an A-B-C: I was great at work today, pretty good at home, and average in my time spent in communication with God. Most people would give anything to score a 3.0.

Bad things happen. Not every mistake or problem in your life is your fault. God puts those things in your life to make you stronger. Stuff happens. Like the time I had a boss who was the poster child for a male chauvinist. Of his eight direct reports, I was the only woman, and it was clear I was going nowhere while the seven other men all had their career track laid out for them by my boss. It was unfair and wrong, but there wasn't much I could do about it. I had to practically threaten to go over his head just to get a performance review after going two years without one, even though the guys were given their reviews and bonus plans annually. I could see that he was too confident and wouldn't last long. He didn't, and things got back to normal real fast. I could have made this my hill to die on and fought the guy at every step, but God told me to be patient. Sometimes you just have to ride out the storms of life until they pass. They always do.

God shines brightest when it's dark. In the days and weeks following my divorce, God showed up over and over again to show me his grace. He uses our pain to teach us more about his love for us, as he stands beside us and wraps his arms around us. In *The Problem of Pain*, C. S. Lewis writes that while "God whispers to us in our pleasures," but he "shouts to us in our pains." I have trusted God more through the mistakes I've made than through the success I've had.

Always have a plan B. Sometimes we make matters worse for ourselves by *expecting* life to be all rosy and nice. Then when we mess up or something doesn't go according to plan, we fall into a tailspin. The first few jobs in my career weren't exactly right for me, but at the time they helped pay the bills and gave me valuable experience in a corporate setting. Instead of complaining about my job or accepting that this was the best I could do, I always kept my options open. Regardless of the kinds of problems you face in life, there are always at least two or three solutions to make things better. Just listen to God.

Attitude always trumps circumstances. I have to credit the writing of Charles Swindoll for teaching me this: "Attitude, to me, is more important than facts. It is more important than the past, than education, than money, than circumstances, than failures, than successes, than what other people think or say or do. It is more important than appearance, giftedness, or skill. It will make or break a company … a church … a home."[2] We really do have the power to choose how we will deal with the failures, mistakes, and imperfection of life. You will never make your situation better by whining and complaining or feeling guilty, so why go there? Pick yourself up, look around, and see that the sun's still shining; you are blessed with friends and family, and things could always be worse. Know that God loves you no matter what. I know the whole "mind over matter" advice sounds trite, but it works. As Swindoll reminds us so well, "We have a choice every day regarding the attitude we will embrace for that day."

Thank God for the thorns as well as the roses. It's amazing what a thankful heart can do for you. If you believe, as I do, that everything eventually has a purpose and works out "for the good of those who love God" (Romans 8:28), then shouldn't we be thankful for even the bad things that come our way? The apostle Paul also encourages us to "give thanks in all circumstances" (1 Thessalonians 5:18). When things go wrong at home or at work, try this simple prayer: "God, I'm not sure why this is happening, but I know you do and that you will work it all out for me, so thank you." This puts everything in its place.

Perfect Is Boring

Remember my friend Nancy from the beginning of this chapter? She is truly someone who had a few curveballs thrown her way. After she lost her husband in an automobile accident, she had no choice but to find a way to earn more money to support her children. She tried to always put them first, but it wasn't always easy or possible. Sometimes she even took them with her in the middle of the night to care for the emergency needs of her patients. But she persevered, never feeling sorry for herself and always rising above the setbacks that came her way. To borrow from the late Paul Harvey, and now, the "rest of the story."

Today, Nancy's son, who made some unfortunate choices as a teenager, is the owner and executive chef at Ember, one of the hottest restaurants in the resort community of Breckenridge, Colorado. Her daughter is a physician, graduating from Emory University School of Medicine and married to another physician.

Even though Nancy was not the perfect parent, her kids are all right.

"Women need to realize there will never be enough time to do everything," she advises. "You can't go off the rails just because you can't do things exactly as you would like to. When you do that, you're observing life, not experiencing it. You have to go through the pain of being human. If you don't, you don't develop character."

Nancy gets it. She learned early in her career that she wasn't perfect, that life is unpredictable, and that it's okay. God always shows up when we need him most.

"When my husband was killed, I questioned my faith to the point you could say I walked away from it," she told me. "But then at his funeral, the minister started to talk about my husband and I stood up and asked if I could deliver the eulogy. Totally unplanned. Of course, he let me speak and it was as if I was floating on air. I don't even remember what I said, but I knew I was being carried in God's hands." The Holy Spirit carried me.

Nancy's life isn't perfect. Neither is mine, and yours won't be either. And that's just fine because we have a perfect Savior who loves to meet us at our deepest need. "God is our refuge and strength, an ever-present help in trouble" (Psalm 46:1).

For Reflection or Discussion

1. On a scale of 1 to 10, with "10" being the Mother of All Perfectionists, how would you rate yourself? Give a few examples to support your score.

2. Most research suggests that women are more likely to be perfectionists than men. Why do you think this is true?

3. How are you most likely to respond to a mistake you've made? Can you think of a specific example? Describe that experience. Is there anything you can do to include God in handling the situation differently in the future?

4. Do you think the church or contemporary culture tends to encourage women to try to be perfect? What can you do to help take the pressure off of you and your peers?

5. Do you feel as if you are held to higher standards at work because you are a woman? If so, who imposes those standards? Your boss? Your colleagues? You?

Are You a Perfectionist?

A lot of professional women are. If you answer "yes" to at least six of these questions, you are likely to have perfectionist tendencies:

1. I practically never leave the house — even to run a simple errand — without putting on makeup and making sure my hair is just right.
2. I find it difficult and frustrating to work with people who are not as competent or fast as I am.
3. When I finish a project successfully, I am more likely to focus on what I could have done to make it even better than to enjoy and praise God.
4. I tend to avoid those things I'm not very good at.
5. One of my pet peeves is to come home and see clutter on the countertops in the kitchen.
6. When I receive my performance review, I tend to focus more on the "needs to improve" rather than the "exceeds standards."
7. I seldom received a grade lower than an "A" in high school and college.
8. I generally do not use self-deprecating humor; I don't enjoy being the butt of a joke.
9. If I make a mistake at work, I'm more likely to be mad at myself than to brush it off.
10. At least once in the past year, someone close to me has suggested I'm a perfectionist.

Antidotes to Perfectionism

If you have perfectionist tendencies (See "Are You a Perfectionist" sidebar on page 202), the following activities/resources will help you curb those tendencies.

1. **Pursue leisure.** Perfectionists are often driven, giving themselves little time for fun or pleasure. Try adding some time to each day or each week for recreation, reading, or other noncompetitive activities. A walk in the park (no stopwatch or prescribed distance) helps give you perspective on life and tempers your need to "accomplish."

2. **Learn the power of saying no.** Just because you are capable of doing something doesn't mean you should do it. Simplifying your schedule takes the pressure off of you to always perform at a high level. It also gives you room to pursue leisure.

3. **Seek accountability.** Share with your spouse or a close, trusted friend that you know you tend toward perfectionism and that you want their help. Give them permission to gently and lovingly alert you when you seem to be trying too hard to be perfect.

4. **Let your hair down.** Do something that seems outlandish to you occasionally. Go to Starbucks in sweatpants and a hoodie. Sign up for your company's softball team even though you're lousy at softball. Purposefully don't do your assignment before you attend your Bible study. Take your direct reports bowl-

ing. Perfectionists often need discipline to be a little undisciplined.

5. **Celebrate every day.** At the end of every day, select at least one thing you did right and celebrate it. Give yourself a pat on the back. Brag to your husband or best friend about it. Pour a glass of wine and savor your success. The more you focus on your success, the less power you give your mistakes. Give the pressure to God.

change with
the seasons

WHEN I STARTED MY CAREER about twenty years ago, no one carried cell phones. Twitter was a word my grandmother might have used to describe the sounds coming from the robins outside her kitchen window. The only "social network" I belonged to was a group of guys from college I would occasionally talk to "long distance." Mail arrived in an envelope with a stamp on it—"electronic" mail was available only in some of the larger companies and only for use between employees within those companies. Airlines served free meals on flights, and when you finished your dessert you could light up a cigarette without setting off any alarms. The hottest music group at the time was ABBA—the first group to release an album on something called a CD. As a young single woman, I found it difficult finding a guy to date who didn't sport a mullet. The Dow Jones average was cruising along at a whopping 2200 points before it dropped more than 500 points on a day we remember as Black Monday.

In that brief span of time I've been single, married, pregnant twice, single again, married again, a mother, a stepmother, a renter, a roommate, a homeowner, a salesperson, a marketing analyst, a health-care specialist, a commercial real-estate specialist, and a chief operating officer. I've lived in Oregon, London, New Jersey, Massachusetts, Oklahoma, and Texas. And I'm just hitting my stride.

The one constant that you can count on in your career is change. If you're in your twenties, forty looks like a million years down the road. But turn around and look back at middle school—can you believe it was just fifteen years ago? Trust me—the next fifteen will go even faster. And just as a lot has changed during the past fifteen years of your life, things will continue to change at supersonic speeds. The business climate will change. The company you work for will change. The people you work with will change. And most important, God will change you. Unlike your parents or grandparents, you will most likely not stay at the same company your entire career and, in fact, may change careers, not just companies. You may get married. Become a mom. Each change ushers you into a new season that will require you to adapt to your new circumstances, and if you approach these seasons with an open mind and a spirit of adventure, they will help you grow and mature gracefully.

Not Much to Balance

When I was young, single, and working for IBM, balance was the furthest thing from my mind. I would have worked twenty hours a day if they would have let me. What did I have to balance? My sparse apartment wasn't exactly equipped for entertaining the book club I didn't belong to. I didn't even have a bed yet! The most exciting and fulfilling thing in my life besides my friends and boyfriend was my job. In this particular season of life you have boundless energy and incredible focus. After all that schooling, you're finally earning a paycheck doing a *real* job. In many ways, you're like an Olympic sprinter who has just exploded out of the starting blocks. Full speed ahead. I did not care about God except at church on Sundays, but for the most part, this season of a professional woman's life is working and learning on the job.

If you're in that season right now, my best advice is to enjoy it. Take advantage of your freedom to dive in and learn all you can about the particular field you've joined. Because no one can be really picky about jobs at this time in life, there's a good chance you accepted a position that might not be ideal for you, but that's actually a good thing, because it's giving you a well-rounded resume. Brad Anderson, former CEO of the giant electronics retailer Best Buy, started out as a sales clerk. Learn how your department fits into the overall structure of your company and approach each assignment as if it were a final exam.

Not to put any pressure on you, but in this early season of your career someone's always watching you to see what you're made of. Based on almost twenty years in various leadership positions, here are the kinds of things that will help you stand out and be recognized as someone who has a future in the company:

Put in the hours. Within reason, be willing to arrive early or stay late in order to get the job done. Regardless of the industry or type of business, deadlines are sacrosanct. If you have a habit of leaving exactly at 5:00, don't ever turn in something late. Supervisors know who leaves right on time and who's willing to occasionally come in early and stay well after quitting time in order to finish a project on time.

Ask questions. If you're given an assignment and you don't fully understand how to do it, ask. No supervisor expects you to have the same level of knowledge as a veteran. When rookies ask me questions, it tells me they want to learn and are eager to do the job right the first time. Impressive.

Take initiative. Back in the early days of fast food, McDonald's reportedly had a slogan for its line clerks: "If you can lean, you can clean." In other words, don't wait to be told to do something. Few things impress leaders more than seeing employees take initiative. Caution: this isn't about trying to make *you* look good, but looking for ways to improve the performance of your department or company. Focus on the company, not yourself.

Expand your boundaries. A friend of mine who was an executive in a media company tells of a young woman who responded to new assignments by saying, "That's not in my job description." It wasn't long before she didn't *have* a job description because she didn't have a job. You may be asked to do a lot of things that weren't in your job description or that you feel someone else ought to do. Do it anyway. Often these are little tests of everything from your capacity to your attitude (1 Peter 2:13–14).

Act like a professional. This may seem obvious, but don't wait two or three years to become a professional. The minute you signed your contract or started your job, you are expected to act professionally. That means dress according to the standards of your company's culture. Be on time, or call in if you're running late. Don't make excuses if you make a mistake. Don't just hang out with other people your age. Find someone who is successful in your company, and model yourself after her.

Stay positive. Shortly after you get settled into your company, you'll discover its flaws—usually from a few naysayers who exist in every company and love to recruit support from new hires. Every company has problems as well as those who love to whine about them. These are usually the ones who've been stuck in the same job for several years. Ever wonder why? Avoid the whiners and become the person who is known to stay positive no matter what (Philippians 2:14–15).

All Work and No Play ...

There's nothing wrong with jumping into a new position with both feet and pouring yourself into it, especially when you're young and single. This is such an exciting time in your life and because it will quickly pass, enjoy it and don't worry too much about becoming a workaholic. Soon enough you'll find that other things in your life will begin to beg for attention. Spiritually, you'll need more than a Sunday sermon to nurture a relationship with God. Physically, you'll need to carve out time for exercise and decent sleep. Emotionally, you'll need to nurture other interests and relationships to help you relax and enjoy life. And there's always that slight chance you'll knock a guy right off his feet with your love for God, beauty, charm, and intelligence—and we all know how much time guys need!

Usually within a year or two of landing that first "career-type" job, you will enter a new season that will begin to require some balancing of all that is important to you. You can't—or at least shouldn't—be putting in seventy-hour weeks all the time (though as a professional, you're always going to have one of those weeks every now and then). And as you continue to grow in your career and experience all the changes that come with life, you will enter new seasons that come with a variety of labels, however, in all your life you will serve God nonstop:

- Christian
- wife
- interdepartmental team leader
- mother of preschoolers
- senior manager
- wife of an unemployed husband
- mother of teenagers
- vice president
- downsized executive looking for a new position
- consultant
- wife of a vice president
- chief information officer
- board member
- parent with an empty nest

I absolutely love each new season of life that I enter. Not that they are always pleasant or easy, but change forces us to step back, reevaluate, and make adjustments that ultimately make life work better. Even when the change isn't something you asked for, there's something about rolling up your sleeves and figuring out solutions that can be energizing.

For example, I took what I thought would be a great position in senior leadership with a company that turned out to be the wrong fit for the particular season I was in. One of my children was going through a new stage of life that required more of my time and physical presence. I hadn't seen this coming, but once it arrived I knew I had to make some changes, which ultimately led to my leaving the company. It wasn't easy, but it was the best thing, because I was able to see my daughter through a time of transition from a senior in high school to college *and* land at another position that exceeded all my expectations.

When I look back on the various seasons of my life, I can see God's hand guiding me even if at the time it didn't make sense. I can also see that each season allowed me to grow in areas I might not have otherwise grown if I resisted what was going on in my life. Three things in particular helped me negotiate each season constructively:

Look for the best in every season. Whenever a new season approaches, focus on the good that will come from it rather than the disruption it may cause. Yes, discovering you're pregnant two months into a new job poses its challenges, but it's also the beginning of an exciting and rewarding journey. I don't know of any mother who would look back and say she loved changing diapers and middle-of-the-night feedings, but she will also say how those infant years were filled with so many special memories. Enjoy the season you're in, knowing that it will soon change. Some women are in such a hurry to leave a particular season that they miss the contributions that are unique to that time (Philippians 4:6).

Be sensitive to how changes affect others. If you are married or have children, any change in your life will have an impact on your spouse and/or children. In the course of just one year, I left one company headquartered in Denver to join one whose corporate offices were in St. Louis. My husband, Chris, left a job that allowed him to work out of a home office and took one requiring a weekly commute from Dallas to the Pacific Northwest. And all but one of our kids were either out of the nest or off to college. It's easy to focus on our own needs when we experience change, but this wouldn't have worked as well as it did had we not sat down first with each other and then with our children to make sure everyone was on the same page; everyone had a chance to raise their concerns and have them addressed (Romans 8:5).

Learn from people in the next season. I have a friend who told me he always tried to make sure he had friends who were about ten years older than he was. "That way, I saw how they dealt with the things I knew I would run into a few years down the road," he explained. Good advice. If you're young and single but think you may someday get married, don't just hang out with young, single women. There's a wealth of wisdom surrounding you in the people you work with as well as other women in your church.

Everything Beautiful in Its Time

I never want to be that person who's always talking about "the good old days" and dragging her feet over every change that comes her way. We've all seen her. The IT department installs a new system that requires some training for every employee, and all she can do is complain. If as a single young executive I would have listened to the women who whined about their husbands or took every occasion to let me know that having kids wasn't a good idea for my career, I'd probably have missed out on all the joy Chris and I have with each other and our family (Matthew 6:34).

I hope I always live for the moment and enjoy each blessing that comes with every season in life. I'm glad I've changed—not that I was deficient as a younger professional woman, but because I know each season has uncovered good things about myself I might have never discovered. Even the difficult seasons have molded me so wonderfully into the woman God has intended me to be that I'm grateful to have experienced them. And I know God will continue to mold me. "God isn't finished with me yet."

A little before my time, folk singer and anti-war activist Pete Singer popularized the words of the Old Testament in a song entitled "To Everything There Is a Season." It's probably one of the few—if only—popular songs based entirely on Scripture. The words aren't really all that inspiring:

A time to be born and a time to die,

A time to plant and a time to uproot,

A time to kill and a time to heal,

A time to tear down and a time to build,

A time to weep and a time to laugh ...

You get the idea.

But I absolutely love "the rest of the story" that appears at the end of this series of couplets: "I have seen the burden God has laid on men. He has made everything beautiful in its time" (Ecclesiastes 3:10–11).

Some of the seasons you enter will indeed feel like burdens. Some, in fact, might be imposed on you and offer experiences that you never would have chosen if it would have been up to you. For every season in life, there is a purpose. God knows exactly what he is doing, even if we're not so sure. The season you are in right now and the next and the one after that. All are beautiful.

You'll see! Just stay close to God no matter what trial you're facing.

For Reflection or Discussion

1. What were your favorite movies, songs/groups, and fashion styles when you were fifteen years old? What are they now? How have *you* changed as a person in that period of time? Are there characteristics and priorities at your core that haven't changed?

2. What changes in your life have had the biggest impact on you emotionally? Spiritually? Physically?

3. In general, are you the type of person who looks forward to and embraces change or is change difficult for you, something you try to avoid? Give an example to illustrate. What can you do to prepare yourself to be more graceful through change if change is difficult for you?

4. How would you describe the current season of your life?

5. Is there any season in life ahead of you that you are worried about? Explain. Is there any season in life ahead of you that you are looking forward to? Explain.

Know Your Priorities for Each Season in Life

Easily the busiest season of a professional woman's life comes during the child-rearing years. Just ask Marissa Peterson who once served as Executive Vice President of Worldwide Operations, Executive Vice President of Services, and Chief Consumer Advocate at Sun Microsystems. All at once.

"I didn't get a lot of sleep back then," says the mother of Steven and Katherine and wife of Eric.

Despite the demands of international travel and a packed daily schedule, Peterson tried to consistently show her family that they were more important than her career.

"I began my workday at home around 6:00 a.m. taking phone calls from Europe and the East Coast," she explains. "That way I could be home when the kids got up, help them get ready for school, and send them off with plenty of hugs."

By being highly focused on her work, she was able to return home in time to fix dinner (with Eric's help), then spend time with the kids, reading to them, playing games, or helping with their homework before tucking them in at 9:00 p.m. so she could have some time with Eric. Then it was back to work for at least two more hours to take care of email, make phone calls to Asia, and prepare for the next day.

Earlier in her career at Sun when she was a VP, the divisional president she reported to called a meeting in Paris to review Sun's European operations. To attend the meeting she would have to miss Halloween and the fun she always had helping her kids with their costumes and taking them trick-or-treating. She asked her boss if she could fly out later and miss part of the meeting, and he agreed to let her. When she boarded her plane, Sun's president happened to be on the same flight heading for the same meeting.

"Why is your boss's staff scheduling a meeting requiring Halloween travel?" he asked.

"I told him that's why I was on this flight — so I could be with my family, especially my young kids, on Halloween," she explained.

"Good for you!" came the reply from the president of the company.

During a previous season of her life, Peterson once quit a very good job because it placed too many unpredictable demands on her personal time.

"Eric was actually very supportive of me and my job and was willing to make sacrifices, but I was the one who determined that this job arrangement was not conducive to building a happy marriage. The job paid very well and it was prestigious. I personally loved the intellectual challenge, but my husband and marriage are more important than any job, so it didn't take me long to decide that a change was needed."

Now in yet another season of her life, Peterson took an early retirement so that she could devote more time to her family, friends, and church and to serve on several public and nonprofit boards. She also has a thriving executive coach practice. Peterson considers herself "actively" retired. Her advice to young women pursuing careers?

"Be very clear about your personal priorities and values. You will constantly be tested through life. Knowing what truly matters (faith, love, family) makes those very difficult decisions a lot easier and enables you to enjoy every season of your life."

set (and observe) your boundaries

IMAGINE BEING IN ONE of those extremely important meetings at work that keep you up the night before mentally going over your presentation. One of those meetings where a potential client representing a significant boost to your company's revenue is in town and needs some more information but only has about an hour to meet with you and your executive team. This is so critical to your company's ongoing success that your CEO decides to drop in as a show of support. You quickly get through the introductions and signal to your assistant to distribute the new project estimates as you stand up to begin your presentation. Almost on cue, your cell phone goes off.

What do you do?

If you're trying to balance your career, your family, and God, you live in three different worlds. It would be nice if when you live in the career world, the world of family keeps to itself. Or when you live in your family world, you are completely isolated from anything but your husband and children. Unfortunately, those three worlds intersect in ways you can never fully predict. Kids don't schedule illnesses to strike when you happen to be in family world. Clients expect to reach you regardless of whether you're in career world or not. Church world is relatively predictable, but just when you've got it tucked conveniently into Sunday mornings at eleven o'clock, one of your colleagues from work calls late Wednesday night and wants to meet you for coffee because she just got some bad news and thought it would be helpful to talk to someone "religious."

I've been in those situations at work where my cell phone rang in the middle of an important meeting, and I always take the call. You should too, but not before having a conversation with your family and friends about boundaries. They need to know that when you are at work, you need to focus on work. But they also need to know when it is appropriate to cross the boundary that separates family world from career world. And since those exceptions to your iron-clad boundaries will change, you need to communicate regularly and often with those who might need to contact you at work.

For example, I always let our kids know that they can call me anytime while I'm at work if it's something important or urgent that can't wait until I get home. They know that even if I can't take the call right at that moment, I'll get back to them within a few minutes. It's important for them to know that they can reach you anytime, that your job isn't more important than their needs. But they also need to understand that you have God's work to do that benefits the entire family, and that calling you just to chat or ask what we're having for dinner makes it harder for you to do your work. If you have younger children in day care or elementary school, their teachers or caregivers usually understand the issue of boundaries and are generally pretty good about only calling about things that are urgent.

Likewise, at work I let my team know that if I have to pick up a call on my cell phone, it's usually because of an urgent need from my family and not just a chance to chit-chat with my kids. If you work in an environment that supports employees who have to tend to family needs, they'll fully understand when you take the call. One time when I was interviewing for a job with a new company, my daughter, Annie, was home sick with mono. It was a difficult illness for her and sometimes she got really down over being so sick. So when I showed up for my interview I decided this would be a good test of the kind of environment this new company might be.

"I just need to let you know that I have a sick child at home, and if she calls during our time together, I'll need to take the call," I explained, adding, "I hope you're okay with that?"

You can imagine how pleased I was at their response: "Absolutely! Family is always first here."

By the way, not every company is that family friendly. Once after settling into a position with a new company, I was in a meeting when my cell phone rang. I noticed that it was one of my kids so I took the call. The body language from my new colleagues sitting around that table was loud and clear: "She's taking a call from one of her *kids* while we're in the middle of discussing the script for our conference call with the analyst?" Unless you absolutely need that job and don't think you can find another one, start looking for another one—which is exactly what I did, and I was gone within a few months.

Kids are more secure when they understand their boundaries and the reasons behind them. That's why I never tell them "Don't call me at work"; instead I explain that they can call any time something urgent comes up, but they need to save their other calls for later. It's the fine art of turning a negative into a positive, placing the emphasis more on what they *can* do rather than on what they *can't*. So when my cell phone rings and I see it's one of my kids calling, it doesn't matter what I'm doing at work. I take the call.

The Power of Saying No

As you are probably already learning, your career alone can consume you, especially when you're just starting out. Everything is brand new and exciting, and there's so much to learn, but if you're not careful, you can turn a fifty-hour week into seventy and have nothing left over for yourself. And it doesn't slack off as you grow in your career. I'm pretty efficient at what I do, but I can almost always find a good reason to stay at work a little longer or go back to my office on the weekend. If you mix in your family responsibilities, requests from your children's school to serve as a room mother, charitable organizations in your community who will come calling for you to serve on their boards, and all the ways your church would like you to get involved, you suddenly have no life. All those good people and organizations own a little piece of you, and all you own is five or six hours to try and get some sleep. I found that if you can pick key areas of focus that provide value during different seasons of life, there will be another season when volunteering for a certain organization fits, although it may not be now.

Most women respond by trying to organize their lives better and become more efficient so they can do all of these things and still have time left over for themselves. Bad idea. All that does is produce more stress. A far better response to your busy life is to draw a boundary around yourself to protect you from being consumed by all the good things going on in your life. According to Patricia Sprinkle, author of *Women Who Do Too Much*, "Our goal should not be to become hyper-organized, highly efficient superwomen; our goal should be to spend most of our time on what we value most."[1]

One of the best ways to establish a personal boundary is to learn to say no to the many requests for you to serve in your community and at church. For some reason, that's difficult for a lot of professional women — especially when it comes to volunteering — because we tend to be overachievers. We also often have this somewhat prideful desire to prove that having a career won't keep us from doing what a lot of stay-at-home moms do, but that's just plain irrational. If you say yes to everyone who wants you to serve on a board or volunteer to run the Vacation Bible School program, you're going to burn out and be of little use to anyone.

It's okay to say no to some of the many good organizations who would love your help. You're not a bad mom if you don't volunteer to be a room mother for your daughter's kindergarten class. Do what God has gifted you to do.

I firmly believe that "to whom much is given, much is also required," but I also try to practice the concept of "high returns," which means I choose where to invest my "free time" based on those things I am most passionate about and where my contribution can deliver the greatest impact. I would not have been a good room mom. I am not creative and I am not passionate about party planning. I am much better at organizing and leading a group focused on learning activities, so I was my son's Cub Scout leader.

I learned to say yes to one or two requests for my time and talent, and no to all the rest.

Take Care of Yourself

As your life gets busier, it's especially important to establish a boundary around your health. According to the Mayo Clinic, the biggest threats to women's health are mostly preventable. In six of the top ten health threats, physical activity was listed as a key factor in preventing or minimizing those threats.[2] That's one reason why I draw a boundary around my exercise time and protect it like a mamma bear protects her cubs. But there's a more important reason why I protect my exercise time and that's because it's as good for my spirit as it is for my body. I'm more likely to be at the top of my game mentally and emotionally when I exercise; I think more clearly and find that I'm more creative. On the flip side, if I miss a workout I am more likely to let the everyday stress of my work get the best of me by becoming irritable or tense. When I head out the door to exercise, it's a good day. When I return after my workout, it's a *great* day.

If you don't exercise regularly and would like to turn your good days into great days, give it a try. I can't imagine following the Lord's Word while trying to balance career and family without the benefits I get from my workouts. My particular activity of choice is running, but if you're not fond of running, you have a number of equally beneficial activities to choose from. Basically, anything that gets your body moving and causes your heart to beat faster is "good medicine," including walking, biking, swimming, recreational sports such as tennis or basketball, and various types of dancing (one of the most popular group workouts is Zumba, offered at many fitness clubs, YMCAs, and even churches who don't agree with dancing!).

Select an activity you enjoy, find the best time for you to do it, then protect it religiously. Especially as you get busier and life becomes more stressful. That's when you need it the most.

One time soon after I signed on with a new company, one of my colleagues called me to set up a 7:00 a.m. meeting. I really needed to meet with him and wanted to get off to a good start with my new company, but I work out every morning and would have to miss my workout if I accepted the early morning meeting. Not a good idea. So I asked him if we could meet instead at 8:00 and explained to him that I do so much better during the day if I get enough sleep and work out in the morning. I also let him know that if he couldn't meet later, I would skip my workout, but he respected my boundary and changed the time of the meeting. I have found that if you explain your boundaries truthfully and show a willingness to be flexible, your colleagues will honor them, even if one of those boundaries protects your desire to have a little fun.

By the way, I always told my kids that the key to good health is to eat well, exercise regularly, and get a good night's sleep. Good advice for you too.

Sometimes we women can get so serious about this balance issue that we leave little time for those simple pleasures that are just plain fun. It's hard enough to set boundaries for the important things like when our kids can call us at work or how we contribute to society. But we all know what "all work and no play" does to us. One of the hardest things for many professional women to do is to indulge in time set aside strictly for her own enjoyment. We can justify our exercise time because it makes us healthier and better workers, but when it comes to carving out time to read or play the piano or work on a scrapbook, we're often likely to let just about everything crowd those things out. Not a good idea according to psychiatrist Lenore Terr: "People who preserve their sense of fun are better equipped to solve problems, think creatively and manage stress."[3]

Even if you love your job, it's still a job. And as much joy as you likely receive from your husband and children, you need to set aside time for yourself to do those things that you enjoy and not worry that you're being selfish. When you treat yourself well, you will be more likely to have the emotional energy and physical capacity needed to balance the things that matter most to you: God, your family, and your career. I started getting massages about ten years ago and it did wonders for me emotionally and physically. Treating yourself well also means taking your allotted vacation time and not checking your email. If you can't take at least a week off from work to enjoy some downtime, you've got a problem. You owe it to yourself and to your company to take the vacation they give you because you'll be a better employee and person if you protect the fun side of your life.

In fact, the more you learn to establish boundaries and protect what's most important to you, the greater rewards you will gain from *all* that you're trying to balance. Your relationships with your family and friends will be enriched. Your time spent with God will be more plentiful and precious. And your work won't seem like a job at all.

That's when it really gets fun.

For Reflection or Discussion

1. As you become more connected with friends, family, and colleagues through things like texting, email, and social networks, what are you doing to establish boundaries to protect those areas that are most important to you? For example, do you let calls go to voice mail when it isn't convenient to answer, or do you interrupt what you are doing with your family to take a call that is not important?

2. At this stage in your career, how do you determine how much of your time to devote to volunteering or other charitable activities? Do you feel as if you should be doing more or less? Explain. What fits with your passions and what you value?

3. When was the last time you said no to a request for your time (whether it was from family, friends, work, or church)? How was your response received? How did you feel about saying no?

4. Do you exercise regularly? If so, what specific benefits do you gain from your exercise? If you do not exercise, is it because you don't have the time or you don't enjoy exercise? Do you also focus on eating healthy and getting enough sleep?

5. What do you like to do just for fun? What is most likely to prevent you from doing it? How could you create a boundary to give you more opportunities to do this? Can you combine what you like to do for fun with time with your husband, kids, or a friend?

The Top Ten Benefits of Aerobic Exercise

Health and wellness experts recommend at least thirty minutes per day of aerobic exercise—walking, jogging, swimming, bicycling, etc.—any activity that gets your body moving and your heart pumping faster over the entire thirty minutes. Here's what you can expect from your increased activity:

Keep excess pounds at bay. Combined with a healthy diet, aerobic exercise helps you lose weight—and keep it off.

Increase your stamina. Aerobic exercise may make you tired in the short term. But over the long term, you'll enjoy increased stamina and reduced fatigue.

Ward off viral illnesses. Aerobic exercise activates your immune system. This leaves you less susceptible to minor viral illnesses, such as colds and flu.

Reduce health risks. Aerobic exercise reduces the risk of many conditions, including obesity, heart disease, high blood pressure, type-2 diabetes, stroke, and certain types of cancer. Weight-bearing aerobic exercises, such as walking, reduce the risk of osteoporosis.

Manage chronic conditions. Aerobic exercise helps lower high blood pressure and control blood sugar. If you've had a heart attack, aerobic exercise helps prevent subsequent attacks.

Strengthen your heart. A stronger heart doesn't need to beat as fast. A stronger heart also pumps blood more efficiently, which improves blood flow to all parts of your body.

Keep your arteries clear. Aerobic exercise boosts your high-density lipoprotein (HDL), or "good" cholesterol and lowers your low-density lipoprotein (LDL), or "bad" cholesterol. The potential result? Less buildup of plaques in your arteries.

Boost your mood. Aerobic exercise can ease the gloominess of depression, reduce the tension associated with anxiety, and promote relaxation.

Stay active and independent as you get older. Aerobic exercise keeps your muscles strong, which can help you maintain mobility as you get older. Aerobic exercise also keeps your mind sharp. At least thirty minutes of aerobic exercise three days a week seems to reduce cognitive decline in older adults.

Live longer. People who participate in regular aerobic exercise appear to live longer than those who don't exercise regularly.[4]

isn't this fun?

IT MIGHT HAVE BEEN Denver International or Chicago's O'Hare. I can't really remember for sure. What I do remember is that I was traveling with a couple of guys from work and we were running to catch a plane. For a brief second or two I was back on the playground in Harrisburg and wasn't about to let any guy beat me, but something snapped me back to reality: a pair of three-inch heels. That's probably why the guys were ahead of me. It couldn't have been the fact that I was a girl because that never stopped me from keeping up with the guys before. And falling behind couldn't possibly have anything to do with the fact that two months earlier I learned I was pregnant and was still trying to get up enough nerve to let my boss know at work. We were still about a hundred yards from our gate when one of my buddies turned and gave me that "Are you okay?" look and I returned it with my "Don't even go there" glare, even as I swallowed back another wave of nausea. I gripped the handle of my wheeled bag a little tighter and shrugged at the strap of my briefcase to keep it from slipping off my shoulder, then found another gear as I sprinted the final steps to the Jetway, handed the attendant my boarding pass, and lurched onto the plane seconds before the door closed.

Even as I tried to catch my breath and not think about what was going on inside my belly, I almost laughed. Here I was a grown woman, pregnant, running through an airport, and a little ticked off that I couldn't keep up with the guys!

Isn't this fun!

Don't you just *love* being a woman and jumping into your career with both feet? Could you imagine doing anything else? I saw a bumper sticker once that had it all wrong: A bad day shopping beats a good day at the office. I want *my* bumper sticker to read, "A bad day at the office beats a good day doing just about anything else." No one forces us to do what we do, right? We *choose* spreadsheets and budget meetings and product development and look-back analysis because we know we can make a difference in the marketplace. We love doing deals or conducting research or filing briefs or managing a team. There's still a little rebel in us when someone cautions us not to bite off more than we can chew. Are you kidding? We want the whole enchilada!

We want to fulfill our purpose through our careers, love and care for our families, and through all of it grow closer to God and serve him wherever we are and through whatever we're doing.

Is that too much to ask?

I don't know where you are in your journey as a young professional woman, but I hope this book has encouraged you to be the woman God designed you to be. It's no accident that you have the intelligence and skills to excel in the professional world. They were given to you by God to use for his service (Romans 12:4–8). Even before you were born, God was uniquely equipping you to do what you are doing right now (Psalm 139:13–16). Everything you experienced as a little girl was ordained by God to prepare you for the work he is calling you to do.

When I look back to my childhood days on the farm, I clearly can see God's hand on my life, providing me with experiences that gave me the skills I now use to manage multi-million-dollar companies. At the time I had no idea I would someday be in a position of influence in one of the largest real-estate companies in the country, but God did.

Just as God guided my steps, he will guide yours if you allow him. And oh the places you will go! When I think of the opportunities available to women in your generation and meet women like you who are so committed to serving God and family alongside your careers, my imagination takes over: CEOs of Fortune 500 companies; university presidents; economists; scientists; entrepreneurs; senators; philanthropists; judges; bankers; maybe even a seat behind that desk in the Oval Office. Why not?

Why shouldn't we aspire to be professional women who can change the world as easily as we change a diaper?

Decades before I was born, a woman named Ebby Halliday opened up a little hat shop in Dallas. Working with her hatmaker, Pearl Kemendo, she designed hats that began attracting the attention of the city's social elite. Among one of her customers was Virginia Murchison, wife of oil magnate Clint Murchison. Although he had made his fortune in oil, he tried his hand at building houses, but they weren't selling, primarily because of their unusual—some would say ugly—design. One day he approached Ebby and said, "If you can sell those hats of yours, you ought to be able to sell my houses."

Knowing nothing about real estate or commissions, she accepted his challenge, dressed the houses up with drapes, rugs, furniture, and a coat of paint, and began selling houses that hadn't moved in months. Today, nearly sixty years later, Ebby Halliday Realtors is one of the largest real-estate companies in Texas. For the past fifteen years, sales transactions have grown by 168 percent; sales volume has grown from $1.3 billion to $4.9 billion. Approaching her one hundredth birthday, Ebby still is actively involved in the leadership of her company.

Whenever I wonder if it's just too much to keep the plates of faith, family, and work spinning, I think of Ebby and the times she has inspired me with her quick wit and seasoned wisdom. She never had the luxury of deciding whether to work outside the home or not. As an eleven-year-old, she sold Cloverline Salve to help out with her family's finances, riding her pony, Old Deck, from farm to farm selling tins of this miracle ointment. But very early on, she decided survival wasn't enough. She wanted to thrive—not just in business but in every area of life. If Ebby could do it during a time when women faced such huge obstacles in the marketplace, surely we can.

Some of Ebby's secrets of success?

Develop a daily relationship with God. A wonderful Christian professional woman, she taught that only through God's guidance will you reach your goals and live a happy, fulfilled life.

Stay healthy. Ebby was a health nut before it was popular and took every opportunity to tell anyone who would listen: "Don't smoke and don't drink alcohol and never retire."

Keep learning. She encouraged not only formal education, but taking special courses, reading, listening, and observing. She knew nothing about real estate when she started, but she became a lifelong learner about the business.

Leave a positive impression. She always urged her employees to treat customers and clients with respect and to have a genuine interest in them.

Express gratitude. According to Ebby, two very important phrases to add to your vocabulary are "I am grateful" and "Thank you."

Choose your partner carefully. List your general criteria for a lifelong partner and take your time finding him. She was forty-six when she met Maurice, the love of her life, and they remained best friends until his death in 1993.

Contribute to your community. Ebby believed in giving back and urged her employees to choose one or two outside interests and get involved in their work.

I absolutely love Ebby's enthusiasm for life. She has perfected a philosophy that I am trying to practice every day: there are very few things in life I can control, but I can always control my attitude. I read recently that corporate presidents consider enthusiasm the most important personality trait. You can't spend even a few seconds with Ebby without being infected by her zest for life. In a brochure advertising an event where Ebby was to speak, she was described as "a dynamic fireball with a sales-inspiring punch that will send you out with a will to sell."

You may not be a "dynamic fireball," but you can nurture a winsome spirit that allows you to rise above all the forces that try to pull you into their negative orbits. God wants you to enjoy life (Luke 12:19).

Not everyone at work wants to see you succeed. Not only are there still men who aren't comfortable seeing women in leadership positions, but sometimes we as women are our own worst enemies in the workplace. There will be days when your lovely little children seem intent on making sure you arrive at work late and look anything but professional. And even the best husband has his moments, as evidenced by what the late Ruth Bell Graham reportedly said when someone asked her if she ever considered divorcing her famous husband, Billy Graham: "Divorce never ... murder maybe."

No one said this was going to be easy, but it *can* be fun.

My idea of fun is to wake up every morning knowing I can use my God-given talents to grow a business. Watching my kids grow up in a home where they know Mom has a job but will drop everything and rush to their side if they need her. Encouraging my husband as he starts a new job as chief operating officer, and swapping war stories with him at the end of the day. Meeting with my small group of other professional women who love God but don't always find the support they need at church. Singing and praising God alongside other moms, little old grannies, men in business suits, and the whole crazy, wonderful assortment of characters that make up what we call the church. My idea of fun is sharing this book with my daughter, who reads it and says, "Um, Mom, you weren't *always* there when I needed you," and then we both laugh at her typical straightforward approach to life that I think she got from me.

My idea of fun is to be the woman God created me to be: beautiful in his sight, blessed with a few abilities he has entrusted to me, and lavished with his grace to cover my flaws, thus making me perfect.

The only thing that could possibly make it better would be to have you join me. Stop in and let me know what you're up to: www.4wordwomen .org. My hope is that we can all support each other in this wonderful adventure that God has called us to. Working hard but always keeping God's guidance first and making sure the family is loved and cared for.

Your Work Is a Calling

If you don't know the name Frances Hesselbein, you should. Before any of us were thinking about careers, she was out there paving the way for us, but she was also setting a very high standard for us to attain. I can't think of another woman who has accomplished more as a leader than she has.

Currently, Frances serves as CEO of the Leader to Leader Institute, which was established to strengthen the leadership of the social sector. In 1998 she was awarded the Presidential Medal of Freedom, the highest civilian honor in the United States. The award recognized her leadership as CEO of Girl Scouts of the USA from 1976 to 1990, her role as the founding president of the Peter F. Drucker Foundation, and her service as "a pioneer for women, volunteerism, diversity, and opportunity." Her contributions were also recognized by the first President Bush, who appointed her to two presidential commissions on national and community service.

"I never applied for any of my CEO positions," she explained recently. "When I was seventeen, I thought I wanted to be a poet. When I was twenty-one, I wanted to write for the theater! But I believe our work is a calling. God has a plan for us, and if we listen and answer that call, doors will open for us."

To women who are trying to balance career, faith, and family, she has this advice: "Consciously look at each area of your life that is important to you and make sure you are caring for each of them. Where you see imbalances or shortcomings, have the courage to do something about it right away" (1 Chronicles 28:20).

She also recommends that you only invest your time and energy in things that are consistent with your values and beliefs. "What's the most important thing to you? What are you passionate about? That's where you will make the greatest contribution. Be very tough about your focus on this and say no to everything else."

What I truly love about Frances is her principled leadership. She explained to me once that she had three tattoos. Sensing my incredulousness, she laughed and explained, "They're invisible. This one here (pointing to her shoulder) says, 'Think first. Speak last.' This one says 'Leaders of the future ask. Leaders of the past tell.' And this one is my life's motto: 'To serve is to live.'"

acknowledgments

THE LIST OF PEOPLE who made this book possible is long. Each person shared special gifts that not only helped me with this book but also served the mission of 4word, the ministry I founded for young professional Christian women.

My son and daughter, Opie and Annie, who took the time to review the manuscript and offer helpful editing suggestions. Every day I thank God for you.

Lyn Cryderman, who guided me through the process of writing this book and provided writing support.

Mentors Bob Buford and Andy Goddard, who helped me crystallize my passion into a mission that gave me energy. Thank you, Bob, for introducing me to Moe Girkins, former CEO of Zondervan, and Lyn Cryderman.

My advisory board for 4word: Betsy Gray, Brenda Buell, Erin Botsford, Hailey Robinson, Linda Lindquist Bishop, Lisbeth McNabb, Marissa Peterson, Nancy Alsgard, Richelle Campbell, and Stacy Repult.

To my "core team" in Portland, Oregon, who started the first 4word chapter: Maria Schell, Katie Reiff, Meghan Dion, and Stephanie Dost.

To the entire Zondervan team, including Moe Girkins and my editor, Sandra VanderZicht.

The dozens of amazing women who graciously shared their stories, which made this book better.

Those who supported and mentored me from childhood until today. Please keep it up. God isn't finished with me yet.

To young professional Christian women everywhere, whose gifts are endless in serving other Christians, their families and friends, and their coworkers.

Appendix

professional organizations for women

Alliance for Women in Media
www.allwomeninmedia.org
Serves women working in electronic media and related fields. Offers job-fax service.

American Association of University Women (AAUW)
www.aauw.org
A national organization that promotes education and equity for all women and girls.

American Business Women's Association (ABWA)
www.abwa.org
Call the ABWA's national headquarters for local contacts.

American Medical Women's Association
www.amwa-doc.org
Serves female health professionals.

American Woman's Society of Certified Public Accountants (AWSCPA)
www.awscpa.org
The American Woman's Society of Certified Public Accountants is devoted exclusively to the support and professional development of women CPAs. The society also addresses gender equity, the glass ceiling, and work and family issues. To accomplish its mission, AWSCPA offers in-depth support in six important areas, including networking. AWSCPA's website has information about meetings and conferences as well as current job opportunities. Some areas of the site are open to members only.

appendix

Association for Women in Communications (AWC)
www.womcom.org
Offers a mentor program and an annual career day.

Association for Women in Computing (AWC)
www.awc-hq.org
Serves programmers, analysts, technical writers, and entrepreneurs. Contact the national headquarters for local information.

Association for Women's Rights in Development (AWID)
www.awid.org
Serves women working on international-development issues.

Association for Women in Science (AWIS)
www.awis.org
The Association for Women in Science (AWIS) is a nonprofit organization dedicated to achieving equity and full participation for women in science, mathematics, engineering, and technology. AWIS has more than five thousand members in fields spanning the life and physical sciences, mathematics, social science, and engineering. Events at the seventy-six local chapters across the country facilitate networking among women scientists at all levels and in all career paths.

Association of Women in International Trade (WIIT)
www.wiit.org
Offers monthly events with speakers, periodic seminars on trade topics, and a job bank.

Business and Professional Women's Foundation
www.bpwfoundation.org
Hosts meetings to discuss issues such as equity, job advancement, and networking.

Commercial Real Estate Women (CREW)
www.crewnetwork.org
For women working in all facets of commercial real estate. Call the national headquarters for local contacts.

Federally Employed Women (FEW)
www.few.org
Serves women at all levels of the federal government, including the military. Also offers a mentor program and seminars on policy and legislative processes.

Financial Women International (FWI)
www.fwi.org
Formerly known as the National Association of Bank Women, FWI serves women in banking and financial services.

appendix

International Alliance for Women in Music (IAWM)

www.iawm.org

Serves composers, conductors, performers, and music lovers. Provides venues for female artists to perform and helps promote their shows.

National Association for Female Executives (NAFE)

www.nafe.com

With some 250,000 members nationwide and abroad, the National Association for Female Executives (NAFE) is the nation's largest businesswomen's association. NAFE provides resources and services through education, networking, and public advocacy to empower its members to achieve career success and financial security. NAFE's website provides information about NAFE, its membership benefits and services, and NAFE networks around the country. It also includes articles and information about business and management, selected articles from NAFE's *Executive Female* magazine, and links to business-related sites.

National Association of Insurance Women (NAIW)

www.naiw.org

Provides opportunities for women in the insurance industry to expand their circle of business contacts and knowledge through association activities such as state meetings, regional conferences, and a national convention. Call the national office to locate local chapters.

National Association of Professional Women (NAPW)

www.napw.com

An exclusive network for professional women to interact, exchange ideas, educate, network, and empower. It provides seminars, podcasts, webinars, keynote speeches, and educational tools and fosters career-development skills that enable members to achieve personal and career success.

National Association of Women Business Owners (NAWBO)

www.nawbo.org

Provides leadership training and a network for women who have been in business for themselves for more than eight years.

National Coalition of 100 Black Women, Inc.

www.nc100bw.org

This nonprofit volunteer organization is involved with community service, leadership development, and enhancing career opportunities through networking and programming. For information on NCBW chapters and programs in your area, contact the national headquarters.

National Women's Political Caucus

www.nwpc.org

Offers leadership and campaign-training programs.

appendix

Organization of Women in International Trade (OWIT)

www.owit.org

The Organization of Women in International Trade (OWIT) is a nonprofit professional organization designed to promote women doing business in international trade by providing networking and educational opportunities. Members include women and men doing business in all facets of international trade, including finance, public relations, government, freight forwarding, international law, agriculture, sales and marketing, import/export, logistics, and transportation. The website contains information about conferences, events, and chapters in the United States and around the world, as well as a job bank.

The Professional Business Women of Illinois (PBWI)

www.pbwi.net

PBWI's mission is to provide a gateway for professional and personal growth through continuing education, community involvement, and a network of combined resources.

Society of Women Engineers (SWE)

www.swe.org

Contact the national headquarters for local contacts.

w2wlink

www.w2wlink.com

For professional women seeking a path to reach their next career goal, w2wlink is a vibrant online community and resource for ideas and personal coaching from successful executives, experts, and authors.

Women Corporate Directors (WCD)

www.womencorporatedirectors.com

A rapidly growing international community of women who serve as directors of corporations with over 675 members who serve on over 850 boards. Provides a unique opportunity for networking, making new friends, and learning from the intellectual capital of accomplished women from all over the world.

Women in Advertising and Marketing

Monthly networking dinners, speakers bureau, and a job bank.

Women in Aerospace (WIA)

www.womeninaerospace.org

Women in Aerospace (WIA) is dedicated to expanding women's opportunities for leadership and increasing their visibility in the aerospace community. Offers networking and professional-development opportunities.

Women in Housing and Finance (WHF)

www.whfdc.org

Offers monthly luncheons, a job bank, professional development, and special-interest groups on insurance, securities, and technology.

appendix

Women in International Security (WIIS)

http://wiisnetwork.ning.com

WIIS (pronounced "wise") is dedicated to enhancing opportunities for women working in foreign and defense policy. An international, nonprofit, nonpartisan network and educational program, WIIS is open to both women and men at all stages of their careers.

Women in Technology International (WITI)

www.witi.com

WITI's mission is to empower women worldwide to achieve unimagined possibilities and transformations through technology, leadership, and economic prosperity.

Women Presidents' Organization (WPO)

www.womenpresidentsorg.com

An organization for women whose businesses annually gross more than $2 million. The organization's mission is to improve business conditions for women entrepreneurs and promote the acceptance and advancement of women entrepreneurs in all industries.

Women's Caucus for Art (WCA)

www.nationalwca.org

Has established a national network through research, exhibitions, conferences, and honor awards for achievement. Call the national headquarters for local contacts.

Women's Information Network (WIN)

www.winonline.org

A Democratic group that serves mostly younger women. It features a job center and a reputable networking event Women Opening Doors for Women, in which high-level professional women share their experiences at informal dinner parties.

Women's National Book Association (WNBA)

www.wnba-books.org

Serves women in publishing, writing, and editing, as well as those who have an interest in books. Offers professional-development programs.

I would love to continue the conversation with you through an organization I founded to encourage and provide networking opportunities to young professional Christian women.

> Diane Paddison, Founder/CEO
> 4word
> 4516 Lover's Lane, Suite 205
> Dallas, TX 75225
> dpaddison@4wordwomen.org
> www.4wordwomen.org

Notes

From Harrisburg to Harvard

1. U.S. Census Bureau, 2006–2008 American Community Survey, "Median Earnings in the Past 12 Months (in 2008 Inflation-Adjusted Dollars) by Sex by Educational Attainment for the Population 25 Years and Over," http://factfinder.census.gov/servlet/DTTable?_bm=y&-geo_id=01000US&-ds_name=ACS_2008_3YR_G00_&-mt_name=ACS_2008_3YR_G2000_B20004.

Single, Married ... Whatever

1. http://wvwv.org/2007/2/22/more-women-choose-to-remain-single
2. Lauren F. Winner, *Real Sex: The Naked Truth about Chastity* (Grand Rapids: Brazos, 2006), 9.
3. National Survey of Family Growth, 1982–2002, Public Health Reports, cited in Jennifer Warner, "Premarital Sex the Norm in America," WebMD, December 20, 2006, www.webmd.com/sex-relationships/news/20061220/premarital-sex-the-norm-in-america.
4. Laura Sessions Stepp, "A New Kind of Date Rape," *Cosmopolitan*, www.cosmopolitan.com/sex-love/tips-moves/new-kind-of-date-rape.
5. Les and Leslie Parrott, *The Love List* (Grand Rapids: Zondervan, 2002), 32.

The Truth Will Open Some Doors ... and Close Others

1. Eduardo Porter, "Stretched to Limit, Women Stall March to Work," *New York Times* (March 2, 2006), www.nytimes.com/2006/03/02/business/02work.html?_r=1.
2. David Popenoe and Barbara Dafoe Whitehead, *Life without Children: The Social Retreat from Children and How It Is Changing America* (Piscataway, N.J.: The National Marriage Project, Rutgers University, 2008), 12–14.

notes

3. "The Only Child: Debunking the Myths," www.time.com/time/nation/article/0,8599,2002382 – 1,00.html.

Finding Compatible Work Environments

1. Statistics cited in Rick Sparks, "Becoming a Family-Friendly Business," Missouri-Business.net (July 2001), www.missouribusiness.net/sbtdc/docs/family_friendly.asp.
2. Kenneth Lassiter, "Owners Create Family-Friendly Work Environment at Nissan," *Topeka Capital-Journal* (March 31, 2000).

Trade on Your Strengths

1. Marcus Buckingham and Donald O. Clifton, *Now, Discover Your Strengths* (New York: Free Press, 2001), quoted in Polly LaBarre, "Do You Know Your Own Strength?" *Fast Company* (June 30, 2001), www.fastcompany.com/articles/2001/07/buckingham.html.
2. Alan L. Sklover, quoted in Anne Fisher, "Help! I Can't Decide on a Career!" *Fortune* (September 13, 2005), http://money.cnn.com/2005/09/13/news/economy/annie/fortune_annie091305/index.htm.

The Facts about Faith

1. Barry A. Kosmin and Ariela Keysar, *American Religious Identification Survey (ARIS 2008): Summary Report* (Hartford, Conn.: Trinity College, 2009), www.americanreligionsurvey-aris.org/reports/ARIS_Report_2008.pdf.
2. Adapted from William Carr Peel and Walt Larimore, *Going Public with Your Faith: Becoming a Spiritual Influence at Work* (Grand Rapids: Zondervan, 2003).

What about Church?

1. LifeWay Research survey, April/May 2007, cited in LifeWay staff, "LifeWay Research Uncovers Reasons 18 to 22 Year Olds Drop Out of Church," LifeWay.com, www.lifeway.com/article/165949/.
2. Julia Duin, *Quitting Church: Why the Faithful Are Fleeing and What to Do About It* (Grand Rapids: Baker, 2008).
3. Redeemer Presbyterian Church, Center for Faith and Work, Vocation Groups, www.faithandwork.org/vocation_groups_page36.php.

Grow Your Faith Like You Grow Your Career

1. Barna Group, telephone survey conducted October/November 2006, cited in "Americans Not Concerned about Their Spiritual Condition," Barna Group, August 6, 2007, www.barna.org/faith-spirituality/98-americans-not-concerned-about-their-spiritual-condition.
2. Phillippa Lally, "How Are Habits Formed: Modeling Habit Formation in the Real World," *European Journal of Social Psychology* 40, no. 6 (October 2010), www3.interscience.wiley.com/journal/122513384/abstract?CRETRY=1&SRETRY=0.

When You're Both Wearing the Pants

1. www.npr.org/templates/story/story.php?storyId=123374274.
2. www.americanprogress.org/issues/2009/10/womans_nation.html.
3. www.pbs.org/livelyhood/workingfamily/familytrends.html.
4. Decennial census and 2007 American Community Survey (ACS), cited in Richard Fry and D'Vera Cohn, "New Economics of Marriage: The Rise of Wives," Executive Summary, Pew Research Center, January 19, 2010, http://pewresearch .org/pubs/1466/economics-marriage-rise-of-wives.
5. Dave Ramsey, "The Truth about Money and Relationships," DaveRamsey.com, August 3, 2009, www.daveramsey.com/article/ the-truth-about-money-and-relationships/lifeandmoney_relationshipsandmoney/.
6. U.S. Bureau of Labor Statistics, Annual Social and Economic Supplements, 1988–2007, Current Population Survey, U.S. Department of Labor, Table 25, "Wives Who Earn More than Their Husbands: 1987–2006" (Washington, D.C. : Government Printing Office, 2009), www.bls.gov/cps/wlf-table25-2008.pdf.
7. Rosemary Black, "For Some Women Who Earn More than Their Husbands, More Money Means More Marital Problems," *NYDailyNews.com* (February 12, 2010), www.nydailynews.com/lifestyle/2010/02/12/2010–02–12_for_some_ women_who_earn_more_than_their_husbands_more_money_means_more_ marital_p.html.
8. Adapted from Crown Financial Ministries "God's Minimal Financial Standards for Couples," *Focus on the Family* www.focusonthefamily.com/marriage/money_ and_finances/money_management_in_marriage/gods_minimum_financial_ standards_for_couples.aspx.

No One's Perfect

1. Jacqueline Mitchelson, "Seeking the Perfect Balance: Perfectionism and Work-Family Conflict," *Journal of Occupational and Organizational Psychology* 82, no. 2 (June 2009): 349–67.
2. Charles Swindoll, *Great Attitudes! 10 Choices for Success in Life* (Nashville: Thomas Nelson, 2006), 17.

Set (and Observe) Your Boundaries

1. Patricia Sprinkle, *Women Who Do Too Much* (Grand Rapids: Zondervan, 2002).
2. Mayo Clinic Staff, "Women's Health: Preventing the Top Seven Threats," Mayo Clinic, February 5, 2011, www.mayoclinic.com/health/womens-health/ WO00014.
3. Lenore Terr, *Beyond Love and Work: Why Adults Need to Play* (New York: Scribner, 1999), 12.
4. Adapted from Mayo Clinic Staff, "Aerobic Exercise: Top Ten Reasons to Get Physical," Mayo Clinic, February 12, 2011, www.mayoclinic.com/health/ aerobic-exercise/EP00002.

Share Your Thoughts

With the Author: Your comments will be forwarded to the author when you send them to *zauthor@zondervan.com*.

With Zondervan: Submit your review of this book by writing to *zreview@zondervan.com*.

Free Online Resources at
www.zondervan.com

Zondervan AuthorTracker: Be notified whenever your favorite authors publish new books, go on tour, or post an update about what's happening in their lives at www.zondervan.com/authortracker.

Daily Bible Verses and Devotions: Enrich your life with daily Bible verses or devotions that help you start every morning focused on God. Visit www.zondervan.com/newsletters.

Free Email Publications: Sign up for newsletters on Christian living, academic resources, church ministry, fiction, children's resources, and more. Visit www.zondervan.com/newsletters.

Zondervan Bible Search: Find and compare Bible passages in a variety of translations at www.zondervanbiblesearch.com.

Other Benefits: Register to receive online benefits like coupons and special offers, or to participate in research.

ZONDERVAN

ZONDERVAN.com/
AUTHORTRACKER
follow your favorite authors